In this fascinating account of God's faithfulness despite oppo          Church,
I am moved to believe God for great things among the people.     Eastern Europe.
He has not given up on them. A new day is dawning.

*—J. D. Greear, Lead Pastor, The Summit Church*

Mark carefully chronicles God's work through the IMB in Eastern Europe. *The Wall That Remains* is an important contribution to the historical record of one of the largest missionary-sending agencies in the world.

*—Ed Stetzer, Author of* Subversive Kingdom

If you are interested in furthering the expansion of authentic faith, especially with a view toward Eastern Europe, you will benefit greatly from the wisdom made accessible in these pages. Thanks to Mark Edworthy's contribution, we can be part of a movement that tears down "the wall that remains."

*—Tom Elliff, President, International Mission Board (IMB) of the SBC*

For all who have prayed for the peoples of Eastern Europe, *The Wall that Remains* provides fresh insight for the future as we witness God's power at work in this great land.

*—Wanda Lee, National WMU Executive Director*

Rich in historical assessment, *The Wall that Remains* provides significant insight as we move forward.

*—Daniel L. Akin, President, Southeastern Baptist Theological Seminary*

From evangelical sparks in present-day Ukraine to vibrant faith that emerged in St. Petersburg, Dr. Edworthy lays a foundation from which he traces the fingerprints of God's missionary Spirit through 100 years of history. Missiologists, strategists, and anyone wanting to learn how the past can tutor us in the future advance of the Church must read this book!

*—Gordon Fort, Vice President of Global Strategy, IMB*

Mark writes a captivating overview of Baptist work in Eastern Europe and presents to us the wall of lostness in a massive area still hungry for the gospel.

*—Jerry Rankin, IMB President Emeritus*

# THE WALL THAT REMAINS

# THE WALL
## THAT REMAINS

Mark Edworthy

*"For Yahweh is good, and His love is eternal;*
*His faithfulness endures through all generations."*
Psalm 100:5

International Mission Board
of the Southern Baptist Convention
Richmond, Virginia

Copyright©2012 by the International Mission Board of the Southern Baptist Convention
All rights reserved. Published 2012
Printed in the United States of America
Published by the International Mission Board, Richmond, Virginia

ISBN: 978-0-9855403-0-2

Dewey Decimal Classification: 266

Subject Heading: Foreign Missions

Editor: Kim P. Davis, Richmond, VA

Cover and interior design: Jana Owens, Roanoke, VA

18 17 16 15 14 13 12 RRD 1 2 3 4 5

To my beautiful family! My wife, Susie, for 30 years of adventure and laughter; our son, Stephen, for an ever-present smile that helps me to see the good; our daughter, Celeste, for a quiet strength that follows God; our daughter, Meredith, for assuming that every door will open; our son, Jacob, for choosing to change against all odds; and our daughter, Eva, for bringing an unexplainable joy to our family.

# Contents

# Foreword

A few years ago, my wife and I were privileged to attend a retreat in a rustic setting south of Moscow, Russia. One evening, we gathered informally around the coffee pot to share the blessings and challenges we each were facing. It was in that moment that I heard words that both startled and saddened me.

"They are giving our next generation of pastors the idea that there is something better than knowing God," said the pastor. This Russian pastor explained how, in the earliest years of his ministry, most pastors operated with "survival theology," indicating that in those days it was "know God…or die." "Our lives and ministries were in God's hands," he said. "Each day required us to cast ourselves on the providence of God in a new level of trust."

But in the closing days of 1989, everything changed. The pastor recounted how the former Soviet Union began to be dismantled in a necessary process that was both painful and perplexing. Not one area of life, including the life of the evangelical Church, was left untouched. Personal freedom was influenced by a remarkable influx of outside sources. The tight-knit, believing communities suddenly found themselves approached by a vast array of ecclesiological approaches, some healthy and others not.

The pastor was particularly concerned about a "not so healthy" influence he felt was infecting the next generation of pastors. He was concerned that in the rush to "grow churches," pastors were becoming less concerned about "growing believers." "Now," he said, shaking his head in sadness, "our younger pastors are coming to believe that there is something better than knowing God."

I am encouraged with the release of *The Wall That Remains*, authored by my friend and fellow laborer, Mark Edworthy. Serving as International Mission Board's affinity group strategy leader for European peoples, Mark's grasp of evangelical work in that arena is both remarkable and helpful. His proven understanding of the culture, coupled with his diligent research, leads him to conclusions that are incisive and challenging. Despite the challenges in Eastern Europe, God is faithful to carry out His plans for the people groups there.

If you are interested in furthering the expansion of authentic faith, especially with a view toward Eastern Europe, you will benefit greatly from the wisdom made so readily accessible in these pages. Thanks to Mark Edworthy's contribution, you and I can be part of a movement that tears down "the wall that remains."

Tom Elliff

*President, International Mission Board*
*of the Southern Baptist Convention*

# Introduction

"The wall is open!" Having put our three preschoolers down for the night, my wife and I watched the evening news with amazement on November 9, 1989. The anchor's words still hung in the air as the camera captured tens of thousands dancing upon the Berlin Wall at the Brandenburg Gate. The physical symbol of Soviet Bloc and Eastern European communism was being destroyed right before our eyes. As a pastor in northeast Texas and student of history, I understood some of the significance of that day. But arriving in Poland less than a year later to preach a crusade, my eyes truly began to see that communism in this part of the world had toppled.

The changes were monumental and unprecedented. The upheaval affected every area of life, from economics to religion, and ushered in a new reality for the millions who lived in Eastern Europe. How would the world respond to the new day? But I kept wondering how the Church would respond.

Months following the electric events of that November, Ulrich Materne, an East German pastor, met with leaders from the International Mission Board (IMB) to give a Christian leader's perspective to the historic changes. He had recently driven to the western part of Germany to see the freedom that had arrived, but he concluded, "The [Berlin] Wall is gone, but it remains in our minds." Outwardly, changes were obvious; inwardly, changes were and still are needed. Many missionary-sending organizations rushed into the fascinating and long-closed Soviet region of Eastern Europe. Expecting a spiritual wasteland, they were met with a spiritual hunger largely unsatisfied by a ritual expression of faith long subservient to an autocratic government.

It may be too soon to assess the total investment and influence of missionaries in the former Soviet Union, but these stories will provide a glimpse into the miraculous work of God and the unique contribution of the IMB. God's grace is evident amidst the challenges of repression and new-found freedom.

As these lines are written, tens of thousands of protestors march in various Russian cities still seeking the freedoms promised with the fall of the Soviet regime. The Soviet dictators were replaced by the authoritarian Vladimir Putin, whose nearly 10-year reign is prompting the current backlash. The protestors are carrying signs: "Russia will be free!" and "Russia without Putin!" Many things changed in Eastern Europe in 1989, yet the need for freedom is still evident. People are still waiting to hear the Truth that will set them free.

# 1

## THE WALL'S BEGINNINGS

At 34 years of age, Dr. Everett Gill was dumbstruck when he suddenly was contacted to consider being a missionary in Italy, a country in which Southern Baptist missionaries had been for about 30 years. Always having a desire to be one, but not feeling like "he had the qualities of a successful missionary," Gill and his wife sought God's will and changed their direction in 1904.

Holding multiple degrees yet extremely humble, Dr. Gill and his wife were appointed to what we now call the International Mission Board (IMB) to be superintendent of the Italian mission, where they served eight years. But those years brought political developments that altered history. Lenin became world renown, the Triple Entente (Russia, England, and France) formed, and a world-scale war was on the horizon. When Germany declared war on Russia on August 1, 1914, Gill found himself in a new role as hospital inspector for the American Red Cross in Italy. Seeing the devastation of war firsthand and the effects on the people of Europe where the Great War was fought deepened his compassion.

It was no great surprise, except maybe to Gill, that God would call him back to Europe after the war and after resuming pastoral ministry in the States.

In 1921, he resigned as pastor of a Baptist church to be reappointed with his wife as IMB missionaries to a continent in transition, to a region where a symbolic wall to the truth of God's Son had been formed well before the Berlin Wall would appear decades later. Showing the love of Christ, Gill would direct a humanitarian aid project for the masses impoverished by war and famine. Hoyt E. Porter was also appointed soon after to help in the relief effort. So as the first IMB missionaries to Eastern Europe, the Gills embarked on an adventure taking place after Lenin and the Bolsheviks took power, Stalin came on the scene, and within a year, the Union of Soviet Socialist Republics (USSR) would form.

Gill's focus was not on politics, but rather God's amazing grace for the surviving believers and what could be done to help them. From things he had heard, there were over 2 million Baptists, maybe more, in Russia in spite of suffering and present difficulties. Gill said that there was a "radiant future in Russia." "I feel I am highly honored to [know] these splendid Christians," he said. "Even in the midst of the terrible conditions—economic, social, and political—[these believers] are making progress."[1]

I don't know about you, but as an amateur historian, I find this reality of perseverance astounding on the part of Eastern European believers. They suffered so much during WWI as did Dr. and Mrs. Gill, who willingly returned to missionary service after the horrors of war and the uncertainties of a new government regime. And this courage of believers and missionaries has not changed, a fact that I can't wait to share with you throughout the pages that summarize nearly 100 years of Southern Baptist missionary history in Eastern Europe. The IMB, having been founded in 1845, traditionally had sent missionaries to China, Liberia, and Nigeria. As mentioned, Italy was next, which occurred in the early 1870s. Fifty years later, the IMB determined to open work in Spain, Yugoslavia (Jugoslavia), Hungary,

Romania (Roumania), the Ukraine, and surrounding eastern territories. The Gills were commissioned to Eastern Europe to distribute aid (interestingly, as IMB missionaries, they partnered with Herbert Hoover, the director of the American Relief Administration at the time) as well as to discover the current and potential believers. The fascinating story continues for these missionaries and ones who followed throughout the Soviet Bloc, but first I think you'll appreciate a bit of European evangelical history up to 1920 when Gill appeared on the scene.

## Evangelical and Baptist beginnings in the East

Don't worry! We will get back to the exciting stories of missionaries, conversions, and Eastern European believers. I'll weave their stories with history throughout so by the time you come to the last page, you'll know the context of what generations of God's workers have faced. Although there will be a thorough look at history off and on, here's a quick overview.

Almost 1,000 years ago, rumblings of differing opinions began to stir between Roman Catholics and the Eastern Orthodox Church, which led to the eventual separation of the Orthodox Church from Rome in 1054. The Crusades would soon explode, which included Christians and Muslims. The famous Jon Hus, a Czech priest, was preaching and speaking against the Catholic Church for a period of time before 1415. That was the year things didn't turn out too well for his physical body since he was burned at the stake for heresy.

Between 1450 and 1920, there was political strife on top of everything else. A Hundred Years War occurred, dynasties came and went, a man named Lenin began his political journey, the Great War hit the world, and the Bolshevik Revolution changed life as the world knew it. A lot was going on to create obstacles for individuals whom God was calling to real personal relationship with Himself.

You'll learn a lot more later about religious history of the region, but you've got the picture for now. Let's fast forward to the evangelical, including Baptist, story.

Throughout the Soviet era and even to the present, opposition, whether communist or Orthodox, charged that the faith of evangelicals was a "foreign" faith. Yet over a century and a half ago, evangelical sparks found favorable ground in three very distinct places. In what is known today as Ukraine, German evangelical farmers were invited by Catherine the Great in the 18th century to work and live on large estates. They were allowed to worship freely but forbidden to proselytize among the Russians.[2] Several serfs were allowed to work the German estates during harvest, and these workers were attracted by the kindness and piety of these evangelicals. Finally, Michael Ratushny inquired and was given a Russian Bible, from which he was taught the plain truth of Scripture. He questioned the village Orthodox priest, who called the authorities and had Ratushny imprisoned. Several others believed and joined the German Stundists. They derived their name from the German word for hour, which referred to their Bible study practice.[3] The group began to practice believer's baptism and aggressively share the gospel. Despite persecution, the group slowly grew.

About 700 miles to the east, an unrelated group emerged from a multi-faceted protest movement in the Orthodox Church. Many dissident splinter groups left the Orthodox Church, and most tended toward aberrant and unbiblical practices and theology. One evangelical strain emerged in the "Spiritual Christians," generally called "*Molokans*" or "Milk People" by others.[4] They received their nickname for drinking milk on days when forbidden by the Orthodox Church. Among this group, Nikita Voronin was the first baptized into this new faith in 1867, and the group self-identified as Baptist.[5] An interesting side note regarding the *Molokans* is the high profile by women believers who were very effective witnesses.

The third vibrant expression of evangelical faith emerged among the aristocracy in St. Petersburg, Russia. Steve Durasoff shared the story of the Russian Countess Chertkova whose little son, Misha, was tutored by an evangelical believer. The boy responded to the gospel and encouraged his mother to do the same. She ignored his pleas until he became seriously ill and died. The young son's witness influenced the countess to put her faith in Christ. She traveled to the West to find persuasive preachers to come and share this good news.[6] At her request, Lord Radstock traveled from England in 1874 and led a series of evangelistic meetings. Some refer to this as the "Radstock Revival," and many notable Russians, including Princess Lieven, Baron M. M. Korf, and Colonel V. A. Pashkov embraced this new, evangelical faith.[7] The Orthodox Church was uninterested in this personal emphasis on faith and would not embrace this new expression of the Christian religion that sought entrance into the established Church. It therefore continued to grow outside the official faith and to influence the upper level of society.

The "evangelical awakening that spread across the Russian Empire in the second half of the 19th century"[8] also spread to Belarus. By the 1880s, the first churches were being formed, and despite opposition from the Orthodox Church and the government, the small group of Baptists continued to grow. Baptist work in Bulgaria was opened in 1866 when 37 German-Russian families fled persecution in Russia and settled in Katalui. Soon German evangelist Johann Gerhard Oncken visited the group in 1869 and founded what many believe to be the first Baptist church in the Ottoman Empire.[9]

Magnus Knappe, a German Baptist missionary, and August Meereis, an ethnic Czech from Russia, pioneered Baptist work in Czechoslovakia in the late 1850s.[10] Early influences among Estonians included Swedish pietists and German evangelicals. The first Baptist church was established in Haapsalu in 1884. These believers were very evangelistic.

Like Armenia, Georgia boasts very early roots in Christianity with the arrival of St. Nino from Cappadocia. The country strongly resisted the surrounding Islamic society for centuries and was finally forced to unite with Russia in 1801. Baptist work was initiated by a German Baptist, Martin Kalweit, who settled in present-day Tbilisi in 1862. He was the person who baptized Nikita Voronin in 1867.

Present-day Baptists in Hungary trace their earliest origins to the Anabaptists that arrived in the 1520s. This movement was heavily persecuted and vanished by the 18th century. In 1846, J. G. Oncken commissioned several Hungarians working in Hamburg to return to their homeland to begin Baptist churches. By the end of the century, the movement counted over 200 churches and 4,000 members.

The first recorded believer's baptism of a Latvian took place in the Lithuania city of Memel (present-day Klaipeda) in 1855. The first church on Latvian soil dates back to 1860 with the baptism of nine adults. The group was immediately persecuted by the government, the Orthodox Church, and the Lutheran Church, so they continued to hold baptisms secretly. The Baptist Union formed in 1874, though official recognition did not come until 1879.

The Lithuanian region of Europe was the last to adopt Christianity in the 14th century. The Reformation arrived but was largely eradicated with the Counter-Reformation. The first Baptist church established in Lithuania was in Memel in 1841. Interestingly, this church sent a missionary, Martin Kalweit, who started the work among Russians in 1867.

The early work in Moldova, known as Bessarabia until 1940, began in 1876. Nine Germans were baptized and in three years, a Baptist church was established.

As in many neighboring countries, the first Baptists on Polish territory were German. J. G. Oncken founded the first church in the city of Elblag in 1844. In 1861, Gottfried Alf established the first Polish-speaking church in Adamow.

Karl and Augusta Scharschmidt were Germans baptized by Oncken in Hamburg and sent to Bucharest, Romania, in 1856. The first baptisms awaited the arrival of the ordained minister, Heinrich Koch, in 1861. The work moved into the Romanian population in 1896 with the first recorded baptism of a Romanian.

Baptist roots in Ukraine date back to the mid-19th century, and the first Baptist congress took place in 1884. By the turn of the century, low estimates stated a church membership of over 100,000.

The period of 1870 to 1930 was designated by Walter Sawatsky as the "evangelical golden age."[11] In no way does he mean that these were persecution-free decades but rather a great period of growth. In the 1890s, the young son of the Baptist pastor in Kiev observed that this was a time of horrible persecutions, including exiles, arrests, fines, and beatings of believers. "Under continual fear of being caught by the police, the brothers nevertheless did not cease their meetings, holding them in basements, across the Dnepr, in the woods, in the cemetery, in ravines, and in the apartments of the more well-to-do brothers."[12] The Stundists were especially targeted, and their passports were marked "Stundist" to hinder their employment and housing options.[13] The Orthodox Church even formed a missionary society with the primary goal of countering the sectarians, especially the Stundists. In 1894, the Ministry of Interior Affairs declared that "evangelicals were dangerous to Church and state activities, and, therefore, the right to assemble for services was prohibited."[14]

A ray of hope began to shine when in February of 1903, Nicholas II signed a manifesto confirming the rights granted in the 19th century to sectarians to freely practice their faith. He further instructed the senate to review the legislation for the purpose of eliminating repression against these churches. The evangelicals, and particularly the Baptists, seized the new opportunity and openness. Baptist writer V. V. Ivanov declared, "This great movement of baptism began from 1905," and later added that it was "a period of rapid numerical growth." Nearly 20,000 converts from the Orthodox Church were recorded over the next six years.[15] Many exiles from Siberia were released and joyfully made their way home. They held public meetings in rented theaters, auditoriums, hotels, and even outside venues. Preacher Vasilii Pavlov described a scene in Kharkov: "When, from the stage on which I stood, I looked upon

"I looked upon the thousands ... who were attending thirstily to the Word of God, and ... it was with difficulty that I believed my eyes that this was not a dream."

the thousands of listeners who were attending thirstily to the Word of God, and when I remembered my own eight-year exile for the propagation of Baptist ideas, my eyes that this was not a dream, but reality."[16]

In 1909, various evangelical groups came together to organize the "All-Russian Evangelical Christian Union."[17] At the 1910 congress in St. Petersburg, Ivan Prokhanov challenged the organization of one congregation in each of the 70 regions of the empire. This congregation would immediately set out to start five new churches, and these would form a local association of churches. Some Baptist leaders even noted upon the map where churches existed and encouraged their members to move where there were no churches to begin one.[18]

Evangelicals were encouraged to move around in the coming years. But we can't forget that World War I was between 1914 and 1918. Some Belarusian prisoners of war had encountered Baptists while imprisoned in Austria and were converted.[19] The establishment of a Gypsy or Roma Baptist Church in Golintsi occurred in 1915.

Countermeasures by the Orthodox Church strengthened soon after toleration was granted by the czar's government in Russia. Yet everything changed with the tumultuous revolution of the Bolsheviks. In 1917, the Lenin-led Communist Party began the overthrow of tsarist Russia. Though the revolutionaries were anti-religious, they were also pragmatists. J. H. Rushbrooke, who administered IMB relief funds (and who in 1922-1928 was the Baptist commissioner for Europe to work with particularly the Russian government to get IMB relief funds and workers there), wrote, "Knowing that the 'sectarians' as such stood apart from the old state Church, [the Bolsheviks] regarded them as potential allies in the struggle against a hierarchy and a priesthood which would naturally desire the restoration of the political system under which these had been gained and held."[20] Since many of the revolutionaries had been imprisoned with the evangelical leaders, a "companion-in-arms" attitude existed between some.[21] Among the first decrees of the Soviet government was the official separation of the Church and the state on February 5, 1918.[22] This separation was already a strong conviction of the evangelicals and was welcomed. Similar laws expressly granting freedom to propagate one's faith and to freely worship were also released. The only major disagreement with the early Soviet government related to the abolishment of Sunday schools for children. Religion could not be taught to children under the age of 18 except by one's parent.[23] The churches continued to arrange for children's events, including prayers, hymns, and Scripture readings but did not register the participants or appoint official teachers. As late as 1921, the Soviets still looked favorably upon the sectarians, even giving farmland for some early attempts at collectivized farming. The communist paper even declared, "Peasant communist associations such as Dukhobors, Molokans, New Israel, and others are completely painlessly internalizing Soviet civil laws and rules."[24]

## A swinging door

The history of evangelicals in Eastern Europe up to the time when Dr. Everett Gill and his wife entered the picture was challenging for these survivors of the faith. Yet, they had survived. For IMB missionaries, the open door in the wall was going to be a swinging door.

## 2

## WALKING THROUGH THE WALL

Everett Gill listened intently to his new Russian Baptist friend, Brother Pavlov. "We need more Bibles," Pavlov stated. He then went on to recount a story to Gill about a Russian Baptist evangelist "who had just come from a community where he had been preaching. The people of that town had never heard the gospel before, and when they heard that this new story was found in the Bible, they were so indignant with the village priest that they were ready to run him out of town for having withheld the Bible from them."[25]

Bibles weren't the only thing desperately needed. Gill, as a reappointed missionary, was learning firsthand that the region needed food, clothing, and hope. So country by country, Gill, and eventually other missionaries, faced the daunting task of being a light for Christ, bringing His truth and compassion.

### Russia

Gill gave a bleak yet hopeful picture of the work in Russia to the Southern Baptist Convention on May 17, 1922. He reported that he was "the first Baptist from the outside world to visit the Russian Baptists after a period of seven years."[26] He saw thousands of starving and sick refugees and reported on several Baptists who had died from starvation. Some were reduced to "eating their old shoes" to survive.[27] He rejoiced that he was able to distribute $5,000 for hunger relief. He likewise noted that, though in dire physical need, the Russian Baptists were still actively sharing their faith and aggressively seeking to start new churches. He was excited to report that Pentecost had been equaled, and "there were baptized in one day and in one place 3,000 souls."[28]

Gill included in his report a visit to the church in Kiev, Ukraine. He met with the pastor, who also served as the president of the Ukrainian Baptist Convention. Though statistics were usually not kept, which helped when questioned by the communist authorities, the Ukrainian Union had over 2,000 churches and tens of thousands of members in 1922.[29] Despite Stalin's reign, the churches in the Soviet Union remained faithful. Gill concluded his report related to the Russian Baptists with the observation:

> As the years go by the American Baptists will learn more and more of the spiritual wealth bound up in those unknown hundreds of thousands of their Russian brethren. When the regular Russian Baptist Union shall have affected a union with another Baptist body that does not yet wear the Baptist name, it is estimated that, probably, the Russian Baptists will be the second Baptist body in the world in the matter of members. For me the most significant fact about Russian Baptists is that they have been hitherto practically self-supporting. Most of the pastors are like our pioneer Baptist preachers of America and the Apostle Paul in that they support themselves by their own labors and give their services free to the churches.[30]

Though money was not requested by the pastors, the IMB and the American Baptist Foreign Mission Society gave money to purchase 10,000 Bibles and New Testaments.[31] Since the Bible had been unavailable under communism, the quickly disbursed copies were cherished across Russia.

Though the IMB did not deploy missionaries into the interior of Russia, it did support three Russian preachers in the Siberian city of Blagovestshensk for several years.[32] Much of this work was in cooperation with the Far Eastern Mission of the German Baptist Churches of North America, through whom the support was channeled.[33] These pastors worked diligently and reported baptism of over 200 new believers in 1922.[34]

Though the IMB had agreed to a three-year relief program in Russia (1920–1923), more funds were sent after the official deadline due to the dire need. The consensus number of neglected, homeless, and orphans exceeded 5 million in the Soviet region.[35]

The open door for work in Russia was soon closed by governmental measures; ongoing work was done at a distance. A Bible school was opened in Moscow in 1923, and the IMB provided some annual support in partnership with the American Baptists and the British Missionary Society.[36] The IMB wanted to give a clear signal of support but was hesitant to give large sums of money, which could be seized by the communist government. With the closing of Russia around 1927, the focus narrowed to Romania, Hungary, and Yugoslavia, where missionaries were able to live until the outbreak of World War II.

## Romania

Everett Gill was first able to visit Romania in early 1922. He described a Baptist Union comprised of three predominant groups: Romanian, Hungarian, and German Baptists.[37] Despite the multiple challenges from political, economic, and religious persecution, Baptists grew by about 10 percent.[38] About 17,000 Baptists were in Romania following the war. Bringing them together was quite a challenge.[39] Gill boldly stated, "In spite of these drawbacks our Rumanian [sic] brethren have made marked progress during the past year. In fact they are increasing more rapidly than the Southern Baptists with all their powerful backing of prestige, leadership, equipment, and a long and noble spiritual heritage."[40]

It is an important insight into the time period, both in Europe and the IMB, to read the priorities of that day. Gill saw that the "principal work will eventually be that of helping in the work of theological schools, publication work, and church planting. For the present we must help the churches to support their pastors, though this is understood to be a temporary matter."[41] In his address to the Southern Baptist Convention the following year, Gill explained the need to add programs like Sunday school, youth work, training union, women's work, theological education, training schools, publication work, and chapel construction in Romania and the region.

When describing the Romanians, Gill portrayed them as "for the most part peasant farmers with many splendid traits of character."[42] They were described as "far superior to their fellow countrymen of the cities who, unfortunately, have inherited the personal and political vices of their former Greek rulers."[43] He concluded that the Baptist brethren were from the country and lived in small villages.

The country of Romania grew substantially at the close of World War I, annexing Bessarabia (Moldova) from Russia and Transylvania from Hungary. The greatest growth in the churches occurred in Transylvania, and the work around the capital, Bucharest, was very small and slow in growth.[44] The Bucharest church celebrated its 10th anniversary in 1923.[45]

But the biggest issue in post-war Romania was overt religious persecution. The Treaty of Versailles had guaranteed religious freedom for minorities, and a new constitution was anticipated that would ensure this freedom. Under pressure by the Romanian Orthodox Church, the promised constitution not only failed to protect against religious persecution but also rescinded former liberties and prescribed harsh penalties for the free exercise of religion.[46] J. D. Hughey wrote, "Baptist chapels were closed, meetings were broken up, preachers and others were attacked and imprisoned, property was seized, and burials were interfered with."[47] Despite the antagonistic governmental environment, the work moved forward with the establishment of a theological school and a publishing house.[48]

Another important milestone in the early work was the appointment of Rev. and Mrs. D. T. Hurley in 1923.[49] They toiled diligently to help establish the theological school and publishing house. They were the first residential workers in Romania and were joined by Rev. and Mrs. W. E. Craighead in 1928.[50] The Hurleys served a six-year term before taking their first furlough. Because of the severe persecution and societal uncertainties, Gill described them as "devoted, efficient, and beloved missionaries. They have suffered much for their work and have proved themselves 'good soldiers of Jesus Christ.' It is probable that no other missionaries of our Board have suffered more for the work's sake in the last six years than these two Southern Baptist missionaries."[51]

Baptist work continued to grow exponentially in 1928. Gill reported, "We baptized 4,525 in Romania last year, the largest number of baptisms we have ever reported in any year from any field."[52] He also announced that the James Memorial School, which was being constructed adjacent to the theological seminary, was near completion. The building was erected in honor of Mrs. W. C. James, former president of the Woman's Missionary Union (WMU).[53] It would house 50 young women who would be trained for religious work among women and children. Two months after the convention, the trustees of the IMB met in Richmond, Virginia, and approved Miss "Earl" Hester to serve as the headmistress of the school to be founded in Bucharest."[54] Miss Hester left her position as head of the young people's department of the WMU of Oklahoma to accept this assignment.[55]

The work continued to grow rapidly in Romania with record baptisms of 4,925 reported in 1929 and over 5,500 baptized in 1930.[56] The following year signaled a drastic change in the work in Romania. Missionary Dan Hurley died unexpectedly on April 30, 1931, after only seven years on the field.[57] His death was a great loss to the work. Political changes also were unexpected as the government abruptly closed the seminary and the women's training school.[58] These closings led to some informal training in homes and churches. Gill reported in 1932 that many chapels had been closed, and missionary workers with other organizations had been arrested.[59]

While the seminary remained closed, the James Memorial School for women was allowed to reopen in a scaled-down format in 1933.[60] Recently widowed Ida Hurley returned to Bucharest and joined Miss Hester in leading the training school.[61] The publication work continued, and Gill reported on a watershed experience regarding subsidizing pastors. Regarding the previous decade (1922–1933), Gill wrote, "We began with overwhelming and unwise generosity, and assisted approximately 100 pastors who had never received such aid before. But we soon learned our lesson, but did not learn of the harm we did until years later."[62] This realization led to a stricter and clearer form of support and material encouragement. I'll definitely mention the challenge of subsidies and dependence later.

The last half of the 1930s would see more turmoil and the eventual departure of all personnel from Romania. Ida Hurley remarried and resigned in 1936.[63] Miss Hester came to the States temporarily but returned in 1938 (which I'll tell you about in detail later).[64] The Starmers, Craigheads, and Trutzas traveled together from the States to redeploy in 1938.[65] Unfortunately, the group would soon be splintered due to the growing pressure from the government and the imminent outbreak of war. Evacuation plans were discussed and soon implemented. The Gills moved from Bucharest to Budapest, and the Craigheads evacuated in late 1939 to Scotland.[66] The Starmers were the last to leave in 1941.[67] Because of his Romanian citizenship, the Trutzas were able to stay (and I promise you'll find out more about him, too). "All of our churches in Romania were closed from December 15, 1938, until April 14, 1939," said Gill. "Many of our Baptist people have suffered imprisonment and fines. Many have been whipped for refusing to worship in the Romanian Orthodox Church. Christian baptisms, weddings, funerals, and meetings have been forbidden. Dark days have been the lot of our Baptist brethren in Rumania [sic]."[68] Nearly half a century would pass before the IMB would be able to deploy residential missionaries to Romania.

# Hungary

The IMB agreed to take responsibility for new mission work in Hungary at the London Conference of 1920. In that same year, Gill visited Hungary for the first time and met with the executive committee of the Hungary Baptist Union.[69] The number of Hungarian Baptists had been cut in half by the Treaty of Versailles, with thousands of the brethren then living in the enlarged lands of Czechoslovakia, Romania, and Yugoslavia. In these earliest days of support, the IMB's primary assistance was the new theological school, publication work, and church building loans.[70] The IMB also provided some pastor subsidies.

"Militaristic and fiercely proud of race, they are a powerful people with a brilliant past, and doubtless have an important part to play in the history of the Europe of the future," said Gill.[71] The redrawing of national lines led to the decrease from 20,000 Baptists to less than half that number.[72] The work continued to grow, and the theological school strengthened with an enrollment of 20, as well as the growth of the publishing department of the Baptist Union. The churches also reported more than 1,000 baptisms for the previous year.[73]

In the mid-1920s, at least three of the Hungarian leaders—Mihaly Baranyay, Imre Somogyi, and Bela Udvarnoki—attended the Southern Baptist Theological Seminary in Louisville, Kentucky. They were leaders in the Baptist Union of Hungary for many years.[74] In fact, by 1927, Bela's father, Adras Udvarnoki, and Baranyay gave direction to the many cooperative efforts that were being organized.[75] Though the report regarding baptisms was down, growth was noted regarding youth work, stewardship, and the construction of 14 new church buildings.[76] Several new towns and villages were entered with the gospel.

The 1930s began with slow, steady growth. The Baptist Union leaders wrote of the very difficult political and economic situation of the time. In 1931, Baranyay wrote to Gill, "The economic condition is bad. ... It affects our church life. ... In the bigger cities this condition is used by the communists for their propaganda. ... The lack of peace between the nations is also a great load on the hearts of the people."[77] That year, the seminary made a change. Instead of welcoming a new class of students, it scheduled three intensive training sessions lasting for two months each. Pastors were invited to the first module. Many attended because they had never before had the opportunity for theological training. The second module was organized for deacons. The final module was organized for youth and local church leaders.[78]

While the IMB had related to the Hungarian Baptist Union for many years, missionaries were finally appointed to the country in 1935. The residential work was opened by two single ladies, Maude Cobb and Ruby Daniel.[79] They immediately began studying the challenging Hungarian language and organizing a women's training program. With the resignation of Ida Hurley in Bucharest in 1936, Miss Daniel moved there to lead the James Memorial School.[80] The Budapest seminary program continued to expand its nonresidential emphasis. Some of the training included evangelistic outreaches in the local cities and villages. Gill reported, "New stations are being opened up where the small preaching halls are packed with earnest listeners who beg to remain and hear more and more. Truly Hungary is 'white unto harvest' while the 'laborers are few.'"[81] The impending war contributed to the spiritual hunger that especially manifested itself in the countries of Eastern Europe. The same year, the IMB provided increased funding, providing support for nationals to fill in the gap with war coming.[82]

Doris Ruth Mahan was appointed to Romania in February 1937 but redirected to Budapest in order to lead the soon-to-open women's training center.[83] Interestingly, both she and Miss Cobb resigned from the IMB in 1938 in order to marry Hungarians.[84] This prompted the return of Ruby Daniel to Budapest to lead the new women's training program. In his convention report in 1939, Gill described the "precarious future" for the work. "The European political situation cannot but have a disturbing effect on the work. During recess, the students of the two schools, women and men, gather around the map of Hungary and vigorously discuss boundary lines and political issues. The disconcerting situation which confronts us is that in case of a European conflagration, we would be cut off from these good brethren and would probably be in opposing camps. It is this fact that makes these days semi-tragic for us all."[85]

## Yugoslavia

Gill's first official visit to Yugoslavia was in February 1922 with Rushbrooke. He noted a small Baptist Union of about 600, which included Germans, Hungarians, and Croats.[86] He also recorded that the majority of the work was led by laymen.

In the following year's report, Gill wrote that "in Yugoslavia we have a small edition of Babel."[87] He described the work among four Slavic groups: Slovenians, Slovaks, Serbs, and Croats, as well as Hungarians and Germans. In a training workshop held earlier that year, the lessons had to be translated into Croatian, Slovakian, Hungarian, and German.[88] Gill described the new opportunity: "The day of the gospel in the Balkan Peninsula has been long delayed, but we are confident that it has risen like a sun that is destined never to set."[89] His report also named two men of Yugoslav

"The day of the gospel in the Balkan Peninsula has been long delayed, but we are confident that it has risen like a sun that is destined never to set."

origin who immigrated to America and there found the Lord. Vincent Vacek and Nichola Dulity returned to their homeland, where they were supported by the IMB and became the first leaders of the work in Yugoslavia.[90]

By 1928, the work slowly increased, and a publication house was established. Vacek reported that he personally baptized 97 people and started four new churches.[91] Gill saw a need for a training center or seminary to train Yugoslav pastors and leaders. The Union averaged three to four new congregations annually and around 80 baptisms over the previous eight years. The membership grew from 600 to 1,148 in 1930.[92] As the Baptist movement grew, opposition began to grow.

Vacek was arrested and fined 500 dinars (about ten dollars) for baptizing a man; the newly baptized convert was fined 100 dinars (about two dollars).[93]

Trying times became common. Vacek reported that more were coming to Christ, but problems existed caused by Roman Catholics. One example concerned a burial plot for a deceased Baptist in a Roman Catholic land. He wrote:

> The Catholics would not allow us to bury our dead in the community cemeteries. Many times, where we have no cemeteries of our own, we have had to call on the civil authorities to help. Only recently we had a burial at Severin na Kupi, where we have a little church less than a year old. The priest stirred up a mob of several thousands and would not allow us to bury the body of an aged sister, the first to die among the little church. So we had to have the protection of four policemen while we buried her in a plot of ground which one of the brethren gave us for a cemetery of our own.[94]

Vacek went on to report that the Union was about to publish its first "Baptist book" in Croatian: Everett Gill's book, *New Testament Churches*.[95] The second book to be published was John Bunyan's *Pilgrim's Progress*. Also reported was a baptism service for 35 new believers that was held in the Severin na Kupi chapel a few months after the opposed funeral and burial.[96]

A key decision was made at the IMB in 1934 to seek a missionary couple to serve in Yugoslavia.[97] The next four years saw the continued modest growth of the Baptist Union, which started two to three new churches annually. The major emphasis of their prayers was for the opening of a theological school and the sending of an IMB missionary. Their prayers were answered in 1938 with the appointment of John Allen Moore.[98] Moore would be crucial to the work in Yugoslavia and the nearby region for many years to come. His fiancée, Pauline Willingham, was appointed in 1939, and they were married on January 10, 1940, in Venice, Italy.[99] Moore worked diligently with Gill and was able to secure property in Belgrade on

September 29, 1940, where the new seminary was started with six students and a faculty of five.[100] Sadly, missionary Vacek died before the seminary began, but his legacy has continued for decades. It was reported that between the two world wars, Vacek baptized approximately 1,000 people.[101]

## Picking back up with evangelical history

The golden age of Russian evangelicals came to an abrupt halt with repressive Stalinist measures, which commenced in 1929. All semblance of goodwill was abandoned by the government and replaced with strong persecution.

Reverend P. B. Ivanov-Klishnikov, principal of the Baptist Preacher's School in Moscow, addressed the 1928 Congress of the Baptist World Alliance in Toronto with glowing reports of freedom of religion in the Soviet Union. Upon his return to Moscow, he was arrested and exiled to Central Asia.[102] Within a year, his school was closed along with the Bible school in Leningrad (present day St. Petersburg). Christian magazines were ordered, reduced by 90 percent, and later forbidden. In April 1929, the freedom of religion laws passed in 1918 and 1928 were revoked along with the right of propagation.[103] The one-time seminarian, Joseph Stalin, began a comprehensive and multidimensional assault upon the churches. The legislation of 1929 forbade religious associations to use the property at their disposal for any purposes other than to satisfy religious needs, give material assistance to their members, and organize special prayer or other meetings for children, youth, and women.[104] The government officially "closed" the two major Baptist unions and imprisoned virtually all of the leaders. Many local pastors were also exiled, leaving most congregations without trained leaders. The six-day workweek was introduced so that Sundays would no longer be considered a "free" day. Churches became creative in the face of this new law. In the village of

> The six-day workweek was introduced so that Sundays would no longer be considered a "free" day. Churches became creative in the face of this new law.

23

Cherkizov, a church leader sent a letter to the members stating that they "also were transferring to the continuous week. The prayer buildings will be open each day, and workers can visit them on the days when they are free from work."[105]

The assault upon practicing believers was often couched in terms of anti-government or subversive language. Stalin particularly enjoyed portraying adversaries of the Soviet Union as *kulaks*. A kulak was a small landowner who hired and exploited farm laborers, but the popular definition was simply "anyone who retained consciously a capitalistic frame of mind."[106] Aid sent from the West to help with poverty and starvation was recast as bribery by international bourgeoisie and capitalist crooks. A group of Baptists trained in the United States was put on trial in Minsk for espionage, and a prominent Baptist in the Ukraine was arraigned as a spy of the Polish General Staff.[107] Economic charges were also leveled at the evangelicals, because they were often the more successful farmers. Their small collective-type farms, which had prospered, were closed and absorbed into the larger collective farms, which contributed greatly to the famine of 1929 to 1931. Also, congregations had to start paying rent for their church buildings, now owned by the state. Church leaders were blacklisted and denied electoral rights. They were denied ration cards, and the congregation had to pay taxes for each preacher, which far exceeded his salary.[108]

The 1930s became a decade when Baptist work was on the brink of extinction. Plans for growth became plans for survival. Since the laws of the Soviet Union were carried out unevenly across the broad expanse of the country, pockets of Baptists were ignored and allowed to stabilize.

## The winds of change

It was not easy to be an evangelical and Baptist from 1921 to 1939. But missionaries like the Gills and national partners pressed on despite persecution and hardships. They celebrated what God was doing in the conditions presented.

In the few years before World War II started, religion was attacked from all sides. A growing German nationalism began to be the dominant attitude and the reason professing Christians had to publicly choose which side to be on—the Lord's side or the side of fanatics like Hitler.

Throughout time, Christianity has persevered, not only when persecuted by political forces but also by religious traditions. That's why I want to show you how the wall to truth was originally built that Gill and others were trying to penetrate.

# 3

## HOW THE WALL WAS BUILT

Since the time Jesus was born, there has been opposition to the gospel. God's people have been attacked by everything from pagans to governments to organized religion. The predominant religious traditions before evangelicals made their mark in Eastern Europe and the former Soviet Union were Eastern Orthodoxy and Roman Catholicism, followed by a minority representation of Islam. These religious expressions preceded the rise of socialism, communism, and fascism and survived, to varying degrees, the pervasive attempts to eradicate them. Although world religions have survived throughout centuries, opposition to true Christianity and to evangelization built a wall that will be torn down once and for all in the future as promised in Revelation 7:9: "... there was a vast multitude from every nation, tribe, people, and language, which no one could number, standing before the throne and before the Lamb."

### Roman Catholicism

Church historians often debate the beginning point of the Roman Catholic Church. Some date it from Jesus's commission to Peter, and others cite Pentecost as the inception. John McKenzie, former professor of theology at the University of Notre Dame, wrote:

> I understand Roman Catholicism to begin with the conversion of Constantine. It would be false to say that the early Church showed no Roman features before Constantine: but the conversion of Constantine was the first decisive factor in the series of events, which was to give the Western Church its Roman character. In the centuries following Constantine, the Greek Church continued to move in a direction, which resulted in its final secession from Rome. Between Constantine and Charlemagne, the Roman Church achieved its peculiar identity with Western Europe, the community of Christendom, and such Roman features as the Latin rite and the primacy of the Roman Pontiff became fixed, but it was not until the Reformation that the Roman Church was compelled to assert its Romanism in contrast to its Europeanism.[109]

The Roman Catholic Church teaches the priority of the seven sacraments: baptism, confirmation, the Eucharist, penance, extreme unction, holy orders, and matrimony.[110] McKenzie conceded that all of the sacraments are not clearly found in Scripture but concluded, "The Roman Church ultimately appeals to its own traditions rather than to the Bible to authenticate the full number of seven, and it affirms that its own history is a valid witness to the belief and practice of the apostolic Church."[111] He continued to underscore the importance of the sacraments as "the major ritual actions of the Catholic Church, and the Roman idea of their symbolism has no real parallels in other religions."[112]

The supremacy of the Church is an important historical and doctrinal position. As early as the beginning of the 2nd century, Church fathers wrote of the necessity of the Church for salvation. By the 3rd century, such a position became more entrenched. The writings of Origen underscored, "Let no man deceive himself. Outside this house (church) none is saved."[113] One of his contemporaries, St. Cyprian of Carthage, penned the well-known treatise, "The Unity of the Catholic Church," around A.D. 250. In this strong defense of the Church, he asserted, "Therefore, you should know that the bishop is in the Church and the Church is in the bishop. If anyone is not with the bishop, he is not in the Church. The Church is Catholic and is one. It is not cut or divided. Rather it is connected and bound together by the cement of priests who cohere with one another."[114] St. Cyprian wrote the often repeated phrase, "He cannot have God for his father, who has not the Church for his mother."[115]

Historically these writings were used as a defense for the fidelity of the true Church and as a protection from the heretical offshoots that emerged in the early centuries after Christ. This self-identification as the only true Church, which was adopted by the Eastern Orthodox Church, was and still is a pronounced barrier and challenge to the work of evangelism and church planting by missionaries throughout the eastern regions of Europe.

The history of religion in Europe was dominated by Roman Catholicism until the schism and the rise of the Eastern Church in Russia. The Reformation would also greatly affect Europe's religious context, but the fruits of Protestantism would grow largely in the central and western regions of the continent with most of the east unaffected. The Reformation awakened a declining Catholic Church and stirred her passions for a stronger apologetic, unwavering response to the upstart movement. The Jesuit Thomas Corbishley wrote:

> At any rate, for whatever reason, the spirit of high adventure seems for a time to have departed from the Church. It did not return until the challenge of the Reformation called out the new crusading spirit of the Counter-Reformation and the Society of Jesus. In the need to meet the criticisms of Protestant divines, a rethinking of the Church's teaching was called for. In that rethinking, Jesuit and Dominican sharpened their wits against each other as much as against the common enemy. In the 16th

*and 17<sup>th</sup> century a theological and metaphysical revival took*
*place in the Church, which, with intermissions, has continued*
*to the present day.*[116]

Traditionally the Roman Catholic Church has viewed Europe as her continent. Belloc wrote of the inseparable nature of Europe's history and the status of the Church. He asserted, "A Catholic as he reads that story does not grope at if from without, he understands it from within. The Faith is Europe and Europe is the Faith."[117] Belloc continued by citing the Reformation for the demise of the continent. He cataloged the countries that embraced Protestantism and concluded, "France, Bohemia, the Danube, Poland, Italy, and all of the South were saved."[118] His summaries, written at the end of World War I, were: "In such a crux there remains the historical truth: that this our European structure, built upon the noble foundations of classical antiquity, was formed through, exists by, is consonant to, and will stand only in the mould of, the Catholic Church. Europe will return to the Faith, or she will perish."[119] Though this position may be a little extreme, it does describe the traditional view of the Roman Catholic Church regarding Europe. The Eastern Orthodox Church would state similar claims to the eastern regions of the continent. These historical perspectives built the context for the political upheaval of the 20<sup>th</sup> century during the formation of the Soviet Union and her satellites.

## Islam

The history of Islam dates to the birth of Mohammed in Mecca in the 6<sup>th</sup> century.[120] Orphaned as a child, he was raised by his paternal uncle, Abu Talib.[121] He claimed to be the final and greatest prophet of Allah and produced the Quran as the final holy book. Roberts writes, "From this obscure and unpromising beginning grew the man who was to found a new religion, unite under its banner the previously hostile tribes of the Arabian peninsula, and lay the foundation for an immense empire which, 100 years after his death, stretched from Spain to the Punjab."[122]

The word "Islam" means "submission" and specifically refers to one's submission to Allah.[123] The religion's authority rests in the Quran, which means "recitation," and is considered the "uncreated and direct word of Allah and is coexistent with Him."[124] The Islamic faith is based on the belief that literally everything that occurs in life is according to the predetermined will of Allah. The basic structure of the faith is found in the five pillars of Islam: the *shahada* or creed, *salat* or ritual prayers, *zakat* or alms, *sawm* or the observance of the Ramadan fast, and *hajj* or pilgrimage to Mecca.[125]

As previously noted, Islam reached the continent of Europe by the early 8th century but was halted in 732 at the Battle of Poitiers in France.[126] The rise of the Ottoman empire in the 14th century saw expansion into central Europe. The city of Constantinople fell in 1453 and by the 1500s, the Ottomans ruled "territories between the Austrian monarchy to the west and the Safavid Persians to the east."[127] The Ottoman empire continued to grow into the 17th century. By

> By the end of World War I, the empire fragmented and the Turkish Republic emerged, and Islam grew exponentially.

1799, the Napoleonic armies invaded Egypt signaling the decline of the vast Islamic empire. Colonization also accelerated with the British in India and the Middle East, the French in North Africa, the Dutch in Indonesia, and the Russians in Central Asia.[128] By the end of World War I, the empire fragmented and the Turkish Republic emerged, and Islam grew exponentially.

## Eastern Orthodoxy

The schism between Western Christianity and Eastern Christianity is like a divorce—many factors contributed to the ultimate split. After Constantine moved the capital to Byzantium, renaming it Constantinople in 330, the political landscape declined in the West.[129] Political and cultural differences continued to grow between the Latin West and the Greek East. Theological points of disagreement also grew over the centuries. Some of these were fairly minor, like the preparation of the communion wine, choice of leavened or unleavened bread, clerical beards, the tonsure, and fasting rites.[130] The two most substantive issues were papal supremacy and the *filioque* clause. Though agreeable to treat the pope as the "first among equals," the Eastern Church refused to consider him infallible or the unquestioned head of the Church.[131] The *filioque* clause was an additional phrase added to the Nicene Creed by the Latin Church, which described the procession of the Holy Spirit "from the Father" as well as "from the Son." The additional phrase was rejected by the East because the decision was made unilaterally and it devalued, in their opinion, the role of the Holy Spirit.[132] The escalating disagreements and animosity finally culminated on June 16, 1054, when Cardinal Humbert, a legate dispatched by Pope Leo IX, delivered a papal bull of excommunication that "anathematized the Orthodox patriarch Michael Cerularius and with him, Eastern Christians."[133] Cerularius responded with a call for all Eastern Christians to flee from the heretical Latins, and the split has lasted nearly a millennium.

Important for the understanding of Eastern Orthodoxy in Eastern Europe are the events of the 10th century. The rise of the Russian state dates back to this period with the solidification of Slavonic, Finish, and Scandinavian tribes.[134] In the 980s, Prince Vladimir of Kiev sent out a team of emissaries to discern the one, true religion. The group first visited the Bulgar Muslims of the Volga but found them joyless and mournful. They then visited churches in Germany and Rome and described the blandness of the worship. They finally visited the Church of St. Sophia in Constantinople and were spellbound by the beauty.[135] They reported, "We knew not whether we were in heaven or on earth." At their report, Prince Vladimir submitted to baptism in 988 and began Christianizing the masses. The government brought in Greek priests and erected church buildings. Peasants soon flocked to the new churches and beheld the beauty of the worship in sight, smell, and sound. Zernov wrote, "The most important feature of the Russian Church, which differentiated it from both Greek and Latin Churches, was the use of the Slavonic language in its worship."[136]

By the 16th century, Constantinople had fallen, and the clear center of the Eastern Orthodox world was Moscow. This shift was first noted by a monk named Philotheus, who asserted in a letter to the Grand Duke Basil the Third:

> The first Rome collapsed owing to its heresies, the second Rome fell a victim to the Turks, but a new and third Rome has sprung up in the north, illuminating the whole universe like a sun. The first and second Rome have fallen, but the third will stand till the end of history, for it is the last Rome. Moscow has no successor; a fourth Rome is inconceivable.[137]

Like a religious manifest destiny, Russia took the mantle of Orthodoxy, which would define not only the religion but also the culture for the coming centuries.

A brief overview of the theology of Eastern Orthodoxy would start with the early ecumenical councils. The Church proudly identifies itself as "the Church of the Seven Councils."[138] Orthodox adherents often quote John of Damascus from the 8th century: "We will not remove the age-old landmarks which our fathers have set, but we keep the tradition we have received. For if we begin to erode the foundations of the Church even a little, in no time at all the whole edifice will fall to the ground."[139] The central place of tradition cannot be overstated when studying the theology of the Orthodox Church.

Timothy Ware was born into an Anglican family in England in 1934 but embraced the Eastern Orthodox faith at the age of 24 and called himself "Kallistos Ware." For many years, he taught at Oxford and was one of the clearest Orthodox voices in the West.[140] Ware explained what is meant by "tradition" upon which this faith is built: "It means the books of the Bible; it means the Creed; it means the decrees of the Ecumenical Councils and the writings of the Fathers; it means the Canons, the Service Books, the Holy Icons—in fact, the whole system of doctrine, Church government, worship, and art, which Orthodoxy has articulated over the ages."[141] Ware continued by clearly stating that "Scripture exists *within* tradition."[142]

According to him, the Bible does not stand separate from tradition or in opposition. Ware admitted that "not everything received from the past is of equal value."[143]

A basic distinction of the Orthodox religion is its rejection of rationalism. Many assert that this is the greatest divider between Orthodoxy and Roman Catholicism, as well as Protestantism.[144] Wayne Grudem argued for an appropriate place for reason and logic. He shared the basic principle that "we are free to use our reasoning abilities to draw deductions from any passage of Scripture so long as these deductions do not contradict the clear teaching of some other passage of Scripture."[145] Especially in Russia, the Orthodox position would stand in strong opposition to any rational approach to faith.

The concepts of mystery and the transcendence of God are key to understanding the theological orientation of Orthodoxy. Likewise, the importance of experientialism is central to Orthodoxy's discussion of truth. The 14th century theologian, Gregory Palamas, insisted that "true theology is wedded to actual experience and not relegated solely to the intellect."[146]

The basic approach to theology by Orthodoxy is often referred to as an apophatic orientation or "way of negation."[147] The argument is made that positive statements regarding God may be true, but human language is too limited to express comprehensive truth about God. In his work, *Mystical Theology,* in the 6th century, Pseudo-Dionysius the Areopagite wrote that negative theology was "ideally suited to its Subject, who is beyond all existence, is superior to the limited benefits of positive theology."[148] In the following century, Maximus the Confessor wrote, "Negative statements about divine matters are the only true ones."[149]

Because of such an approach to theology, many argue that a clear Orthodox systematic theology is difficult, if not impossible, to find. The exception often cited is the *Exposition of the Orthodox Faith* by John of Damascus in the 8th century.[150] This ancient Father wrote voluminous pages on matters like heresy, angels, property, the Trinity, virginity, and hundreds of other doctrines. In contrast, Timothy Ware had presented Orthodoxy under seven headings. These are God as Mystery, Trinity, Creator, Man, Spirit, Prayer, and Eternity.[151] As mystery, God is ultimately transcendent though somehow near. Ware summarized that God is: "Unknowable in His essence, yet known in His energies; beyond and above all that we can think or express, yet closer to us than our own heart. Through the apophatic way we smash in pieces all the idols or mental images that we form of Him, for we know that all are unworthy of His surpassing greatness."[152] A major emphasis on the Trinitarian aspect of God is central to Orthodoxy. The decrees of the ancient councils reaffirm this foundational doctrine. Ware underscored that one cannot logically prove the Trinity. He continued, "The threeness of God is something given or revealed to us in Scripture, in the Apostolic Tradition, and in the experience of the saints throughout the centuries. All that we can do is to *verify* this given fact through our own life of prayer."[153]

God as creator is another pillar in the view of Orthodoxy. Ware clarified: "The purpose of the creation doctrine, then, is not to ascribe a chronological starting point to the world, but to affirm that at this present moment, as at all moments, the world depends for its existence upon God."[154] Again, the sovereignty and transcendence of God is underscored. In his discussion of God as man, Ware highlighted the love of God in redemption. He wrote that "there was a cross in the heart of God before there was one planted outside Jerusalem."[155] When discussing God as Spirit, Ware returned to the centrality of the Trinity. He spoke of two firm truths regarding the Spirit: He is a person, and He is both coequal and coeternal with the Father and the Son.[156]

God is sometimes described as prayer in Orthodoxy. Vasilii Rozanov wrote, "There is no life without prayer. Without prayer there is only madness and horror. The soul of Orthodoxy consists in the gift of prayer."[157] In his discussion of God as Eternity, Ware addressed the Second Coming. He wrote, "Eternity signifies unending progress, a never ceasing advance."[158] Even in his theological writings, Ware described more the experience of the faith than doctrinal truths or theological abstracts. These have been merely representative of a system wedded to mystical belief and ancient tradition.

The Russian Orthodox Church was not exempt from suffering under communism. The communists often attacked the Church for its wealth and apparent lack of concern for the poor. The Church's clear tie with the czarist government also prompted persecution from the new power structure. Ultimately, it was too powerful for the communists to allow to coexist. Thousands of churches and monasteries were closed during the reign of Stalin. On the eve of World War II, there were less than 300 churches in all of the Soviet Union.[159] Periods of advance and setbacks marked the decades following World War II.

> Thousands of churches and monasteries were closed during the reign of Stalin.

## Communism's mark

The religious contexts in Eastern Europe at the time of communism's fall were diverse and complex. Many missionaries were ill-prepared for this complexity, which contributed to some false starts and delayed successes in the early days. The official communist line of atheism was largely believed, though most people in Eastern Europe continued to carry a belief in God. One missionary in Romania wrote, "I thought that I was going to reach an atheistic country; in fact, I discovered a people whose faith was very important to them. Many said to me in conversation, 'To provide for my family, I had to be in the Communist Party, and therefore had to sign the statement that I believe there is no God. But in my heart I always believed.'"[160]

The difference between a ritual faith that may have endured several generations under communism and a biblical faith shared by missionaries was pronounced but sometimes unclear to the host cultures. Often, the very foundation of their faith that helped Eastern Europeans weather the fierce storm of communism was being confronted by newly arrived Christian missionaries who rarely knew the history and often lacked appreciation for the people's depth of faith. Yet, despite the challenges of different starting points, many missionaries effectively engaged the emerging cultures with strong biblical teaching and fruitful service.

Much more than traditional religions or communism would affect the coming period of time. A wall to close out the gospel would come in the form of dictators, war, and fear.

# 4

## THE WALL BECOMES VISIBLE

Herr Schmidt, secretary for the German Baptists, traveled through Germany in the late 1930s having the audacity to encourage Baptists to show allegiance to the growing nationalism and the Nazi way of thinking. Everett Gill was sick about this *Drang nach Oaten,* the push toward nationalism. Whether they wanted to or not, and under the direction of Schmidt, Baptists were led to play the government game. Gill had even heard of a German missionary who had been arrested in Africa for espionage but freed on his word of honor. He told the judge, "I must let you know that first of all I am a German, and then a Christian."[161] People were selling out due to pressure.

It wouldn't be long before a book would be circulated, *Gott und Volk*, that stated, "We Germans have been called upon by fate to be the first to break with Christianity ... A thousand bonds tie us to the Christian belief, but one blow will make us free ... thank God that He sent the Fuhrer ... The age of Christian civilization is past. Only German civilization has anything to say. Therefore we cannot be Christians ... We want to fill [cathedrals] with a new spirit. We want to proclaim a new faith in them ... We want to educate [the youth] to tear the faith of Christianity out of their hearts: only Germany has a place there."[162] The Nazis had plans to spread this ideology over Eastern Europe as they planned to conquer it.

Gill saw that the protection they had for 20 years was breaking down. He expected that widespread war was on the horizon. This prelude to World War II brought challenges to the spread of the gospel. As nationalism grew rampant, Hitler's rise to power brought far reaching consequences to the political and religious future of Eastern Europe. By 1936, Hitler had ordered the reoccupation of the Rhineland, a region along the Rhine River, and sent troops to aid Franco in Spain in 1938.[163] Later that year, Germany annexed the Sudetenland from Czechoslovakia.[164] Hitler's aggression and ambition finally culminated with Germany's invasion of Poland on September 1, 1939.[165] On September 3, Great Britain and France declared war on Germany, and the biggest war in history commenced.[166] Names of countries, borders, and governments were changing faster than anyone could keep up with. Poland was divided between Nazi Germany and the USSR in 1939 after the German army invaded it. Of 7,000 Baptists reported in Poland in 1921, only 1,000 remained by war's end.[167] Latvia, Estonia, and Lithuania were forced to incorporate into the USSR a year later.

At the time of all the turmoil, the elderly Dr. and Mrs. Gill retired from the IMB in 1939. They had raised three children in Eastern Europe (one who later served as IMB secretary for Latin America). After eight years in Italy and 18 years of service in Eastern Europe, the place they loved so much seemed to be deteriorating right before their eyes. Known as "a big man in his sympathy and understanding," a world citizen, an author, and a man who showed himself approved unto God,[168] it was no wonder that in the present conditions, he believed that Christians had come to a time "deadly for us."[169]

## World War II

Two noteworthy announcements were made at the IMB trustee meeting on December 22, 1941. The first was the pledge of the IMB to send two representatives to the upcoming Baptist World Emergency Committee meeting in Atlanta and to "cooperate to the fullest extent with the south-wide committee in raising whatever sum may be necessary for the whole program of relief in all lands where the Mission has work."[170] The second was a declaration to issue a special edition of *The Commission*, the IMB magazine for Southern Baptist constituents, the following month, "containing the name, picture, and address of all missionaries in war-torn lands, with the appeal that all of our people join earnestly in daily prayer for the preservation and relief of all these missionaries."[171] One hundred and twenty-nine missionaries were affected by WWII, most in China. Nine were in the Philippines, 15 were in the Hawaiian Islands (not a U. S. state yet), and one single, male missionary was in Japan. Only five IMB missionaries remained in all of Europe: Mr. and Mrs. John Allen Moore and Ruby Daniel in Budapest, Hungary; and Mr. and Mrs. Roy Starmer in Bucharest, Romania. (The missionary we know as Miss Hester was in the States but as promised, you're going to love to hear more about her in a minute.) When *The Commission* came out in January 1942, there was a clear call for all Baptists in the South to "pray fervently, earnestly, and continuously for the safety and protection of our blessed and sacrificial missionaries." The article went on to show the intensity of the appeal by saying, "We have come to the supreme hour of utter dependence upon God for the saving and keeping of these 129 missionaries whom He has called and consecrated to the high and holy task of making known His way of eternal life to the pagan and heathen peoples, now in the grip of insane and suicidal war."[172]

Interestingly enough, during the early 40s, Stalin relaxed government control and persecution of the Church. He had enough to think about with Hitler. IMB work there had practically ended years earlier due to the restrictions he enacted. But with these laws relaxed, pockets of revival broke out in many places. With the IMB focus in Eastern Europe during the war being Romania, Hungary, and Yugoslavia, since Russia had been closed to ministry in the 30s, I find it very interesting to look at the work in each of these three countries in detail. However, Baptists in Russia were "very much alive and growing rapidly." Eight Russian Baptists and seven other evangelical Christians had been able to send a letter pleading for Baptists all over the world to join with them for a day of prayer on June 14, 1942, for "the speedy approach of the hour of triumph of the great principles of freedom and Christianity over the man-hating ... powers of Fascism." They reported that "their hearts are occupied with the fate of all the peoples who have been hurled by the evil will of Hitler into the horror of war." Baptists in America responded to the call to prayer, and thousands of Bibles were sent for prisoners of war in Geneva and for war refugees escaping to surrounding countries.

## Romania

A decree was sent out in the late 30s that all Baptist churches would be shut down in Romania. Before this, Miss Earl Hester had gone back to the States temporarily and found love unexpectedly and coincidentally with a Romanian student studying at a seminary in America. She married Petre Trutza in 1937, and he was appointed by the IMB to serve with her in his home country. After returning to Romania in 1938 and seeing great persecution and suffering as a result of the war, the couple came to the States in March 1941, and she told a story to Southern Baptists of when church doors were forced to close.

"The evening before the date set for official closing and sealing, we met for a last prayer service together. Such prayers as ascended that evening from the hearts of our persecuted brethren! They prayed for the spirit of faithfulness. They prayed for the young people who would be tempted to drift away while God's house was closed. They pled for the people who had recently heard the Gospel and would now be left without further instruction." Mrs. Trutza went on to tell of military take-overs, which flooded refugees into Bucharest. Her husband, a Romanian, was called up as a soldier. They were bewildered when the Romanian king was exiled and the Iron Guards took control. "Prayer came like breathing. We so much needed comfort and hope!" She said that they and their Christian brothers "remembered the frailty of life and pledged Him our service."[173]

While the Germans entered Poland from the west, Russia began to usurp territories in the east. It not only entered Poland but also reclaimed Bessarabia (Moldova) in 1940, which had been given to Romania at Versailles.[174] The rapid growth of the Baptists was immediately halted by the occupiers. An earthquake hit Bucharest the same year, partially damaging the seminary.[175] On December 11, 1941, the IMB vice president, George Sadler, wired a message to the Starmers in Romania and the Moores in Hungary: "BOARD AUTHORIZES YOU AND DANIEL PLACE YOURSELVES UNDER DIRECTION AMERICAN CONSUL RETURN AMERICA IF ADVISABLE EFFORTS BEING MADE IN WASHINGTON TO ARRANGE FINANCES."[176] These couples eventually were able to leave until further notice.

In 1943, IMB properties were confiscated by the Romanian authorities.[177] These properties would change hands many times over the following decades.

But on October 30, 1944, Baptists were given the same legal status as other religious institutions and the designation as a "historic cult."[178] Many churches were able to reopen, and a congress for all Baptist churches was held in Arad in October 1945.[179] More than 500 delegates attended, and 3,500 attended the closing session.[180] But that freedom would end eventually for decades to come.

## Hungary

The prophetic words of Everett Gill were confirmed as the war began, and Hungary joined the Axis powers. As in nearby countries, Hungary experienced widespread devastation and intense poverty under the rule of the Germans. A large portion of Transylvania returned to Hungary at the beginning of the war but was relinquished again at the war's conclusion.[181] When hostilities began, many of the missionaries fled to Budapest. In the IMB trustee report in early 1942, the record noted the evacuation of remaining personnel: John Allen and Pauline Moore along with Ruby Daniel.[182]

Contact with the Hungarian Baptist Union was almost nonexistent through the war years. Word was received of difficult circumstances and food shortages, but the extent of the destruction was not known until after the war. A message was sent from the seminary that it had been bombed:

> That day, Bela lost his wife, his friends, his home, and his belongings.

"Lost all belongings in Baptist seminary. Please send help."[183] In the bombing, a shell hit the seminary apartment where the seminary president, Bela Udvarnoki (mentioned earlier) and his wife, Gladys, who was born in Mississippi, lived. Gladys died immediately, along with three people who were visiting. That day, Bela lost his wife, his friends, his home, and his belongings.[184] (A few years later, IMB missionary Ruby Daniel would fall in love, resign from the IMB, and be married in 1947 to Bela.)[185]

## Yugoslavia

Yugoslavia was the last country entered by the IMB prior to World War II, and the missionaries had closer contact with this country in the post-war years than with Romania or Hungary. As I've mentioned, the work in Yugoslavia had been led by a national, Vincent Vacek, until the arrival of new missionaries, John Allen and Pauline Moore. Moore started the long-awaited theological school in September 1940.[186] In less than a year, the Moores were forced to escape by boat up the Danube to Budapest.[187]

Mrs. Moore and some belongings were transported to the river while her husband finished up several things at their apartment before rushing to join her. On his way, he was stopped at a checkpoint by two guards, one German and one Serbian. He had no identification with him and explained that he was a foreigner who worked with a Christian organization. They did not believe him and pointed him toward a prisoner train car. Desperately, Moore finally reached into the pocket of his jacket and found a life insurance policy. Silently breathing a prayer, he showed the guards the policy and confidently explained that this spoke of his job assignment. Both guards were too embarrassed to admit that they did not understand English so they took a cursory look at the policy and agreed that his papers were in order. They let him pass.[188] He joined his wife, barely making it.

The Moores stayed in Budapest about six months before they were escorted to Lisbon on a train guarded by the American Legation.[189] They took a boat from Lisbon to Cuba, where they stayed for a while before returning to the States for the rest of the war. He earned his Ph.D. at Southern Baptist Theological Seminary in Louisville, Kentucky, upon his return.[190]

## The end of World War II

With WWII ending in 1945 and liberation from Germany occurring for the USSR, Stalin unleashed his strength against anything and anyone who would threaten his power. Persecution and arrests of dissidents became common. After the war, it took quite a while to figure out exactly what had happened to Baptists and the work. The outbreak of the war changed the nature of the work.

The Moores, who were in the States when the war was over, were seconded to the United Nations Relief and Rehabilitation Administration and, along with J. D. Hughey, Jr., went to Egypt to work with Yugoslav refugees in early 1945.[191] At the same time, Everett Gill, though retired, sought permission to visit the work in Hungary, Romania, and Yugoslavia. He was denied a visa to the first two countries but was able to visit Yugoslavia. His impression upon arriving in Belgrade was deeply moving: "Never have I felt such an atmosphere; never have I seen such evidence of misery as I felt and saw in Serbia and Croatia. It was as if horrible tentacles had reached out and taken millions of unwilling peoples into their grasp. It was as if invisible forces had done their best to crush every iota of freedom and peace out of a liberty-loving people. It is estimated that 90 percent of the country has been communized and that thousands of heads have gone off and thousands sent to concentration camps in the process."[192] Yet, "revival fires" were burning brightly in several parts of the country. About 200 baptisms were recorded annually during the war.[193] Seminary classes had recently resumed with nine students enrolled.

The Moores were not allowed to re-enter Yugoslavia, so they returned in 1945 to the United States from their work in Egypt with refugees to await further assignment overseas. While teaching at Baylor University, Moore received an urgent letter from a Yugoslav pastor in 1948:

> *We are again in great difficulties. Please, dear brother, you write Dr. Sadler in my name. I must not write him. Both the letters I write and those I receive go through censorship; they are photographed and filed with OZNA (secret police). OZNA has forbidden me to travel. Brother Simic was imprisoned by OZNA eight days ago, and I am expecting it for myself any day. The newspapers here write that President Truman is a Baptist; they consider us spies.[194]*

The communist government tightened its grip in Hungary, which made it impossible for IMB personnel to even visit the brethren. Financial assistance was sent to the Baptist Union along with correspondence of encouragement. Even these steps became problematic as the IMB received a note from Imre Somogyi of the Union asking that he no longer receive money from the United States but arrangements be made to forward funds through Sweden. Dr. Somogyi recommended that no mail be sent in his name and that the sending of parcels to Hungarian Baptists be discontinued."[195] Funds and gifts were only occasionally sent due to these dangerous restrictions.

In the IMB convention report in 1949, an update of the support provided to the Hungarian Union was included:

*The barriers, which separate Hungary from the outside world, have become almost impenetrable. Recent arrest in Hungary of two Americans has placed this normally friendly country practically out-of-bounds to our citizenry. Late last fall we were able to send Hungary money for our work in general, typewriters for some of our leading pastors, a mimeograph, a supply of books with modern kitchen equipment for the seminary.[196]*

Contact was very sporadic with the Union. Occasional letters would get through with news of the seminary enrollment or the starting of a new church. When one of the pastors was able to travel abroad, which was very rare, a meeting was often arranged. The random searches and confiscation of correspondence added to the uncertainty of the situation. Word arrived in 1952 that Somogyi had died but that the Union continued to faithfully move forward.[197] It would be until the 1970s before things settled down there for believers.

The biggest IMB influence upon the work in the region during the 1940s came with the establishment of the International Baptist Theological Seminary in Switzerland in 1949.[198] After nearly 30 years of discussions, the IMB purchased property in Ruschlikon, and the dream of a European seminary was a reality. Classes were first held in September 1949 with students attending from 13 different countries.[199] Moore was asked to be the registrar and a professor. Most of the professors were from the United States, though some were from Europe. The seminary would be a major investment of the IMB for many years.

Though all three of the Eastern European countries engaged by the IMB were behind the "Iron Curtain," Yugoslavia's government had a greater openness to the West than the governments of Romania and Hungary. In an IMB report to the trustees in 1949, Secretary George Sadler explained that the Christians in Yugoslavia had fewer restraints than their neighbors to the east. He continued that "the superior position of Yugoslav Christians is probably explained by Tito's refusal to fit into a pattern outlined by the Kremlin, not his friendly attitude toward Christians."[200] The Moores tested this new openness and were able to secure travel visas into Yugoslavia, where they enjoyed the Christmas holidays in 1950. They were welcomed by the brethren and noted the scarcity of goods in the noncommunist stores. They took a letter with them to deliver to Sadler inviting him to visit the Baptist Union. Sadler was able to accept the invitation in 1952 and enjoyed a 12-day trip in the country.[201]

Stalin died in March 1953, and Nikita Khrushchev succeeded him. In November 1954, Khrushchev issued the decree, "On Mistakes in the Conduct of Scientific-Atheist Propaganda among the Population."[202] This decree admitted gross errors in the party's attack on religious associations. These immediate years are often called "the thaw" after Stalin's freeze. After a season of growing freedom and growth, evangelicals again experienced the government's sharp crackdown in the early 1960s. In 1961, over 300 Baptist churches were closed and over half of all of the Union churches would be shuttered within three years.[203] Khrushchev boasted publicly that the party would "take God by the beard," and he would ultimately show the last "[Soviet] Christian on television by 1980."[204] Waves of persecution resulted from Khrushchev's determination to transition from socialism to true communism. In the state-run paper, *Pravda*, an atheistic writer observed, "The closing of a parish does not make atheists of the believers. On the contrary, it attracts people all the more to religion and in addition embitters their hearts."[205] His commentary proved true.

An unfortunate result of persecution by the state was a resultant split among the evangelicals, particularly the Baptists. The government required registration and gave parameters for denominations to accept. The All-Union Council of

Evangelical Christian-Baptists sought to comply with many of these requirements out of respect for the authorities and the desire to remain free to persevere and ultimately to spread the gospel. This Union sent their new statute and secret letter of instructions to the senior pastors throughout the country in 1960. This letter "warned about 'unhealthy missionary tendencies,' asserting that a membership drive 'must be decisively terminated.' Baptism of young people between 18 and 30 must be kept 'to a complete minimum.'"[206] The backlash ultimately led to the formation of the Council of Churches of Evangelical Christian-Baptists, which was sometimes referred to as the "initiators" or *Initsiativniki* in Russian or even the Reformed Baptists.[207] While persecution was experienced by both unions, the government seemed more intent to punish the unregistered and more radical splinter group. The divided body of Baptists would persist for many decades.

Let me take a minute to explain more about the concept of true communism. Communism has been called a worldview, religion, philosophy, political conviction, economic necessity, and more by its adherents and opponents. David Noebel wrote that communism has "a theology, philosophy, an ethics, a politics, and an economics."[208] He concluded that it has "a total religious worldview."[209] Though opinions vary whether to classify communism as a religion or not, Nobel argued well that it has a faith element and some religious connotations. Communism is defined as "a theory or system of social organization based on the holding of all property in common."[210] The communistic system in the Soviet Union was far more complex than this simple description and had a belief framework that rejected the existing majority faith systems. In his voluminous writings, Lenin commented on a correspondence from Engels to Dühring: "The philosophical basis of Marxism, as Marx and Engels repeatedly declared, is dialectical materialism. ... a materialism which is absolutely atheistic and positively hostile to all religion."[211] He continued, "We must combat religion, that is the ABC of all materialism, and consequently of Marxism."[212]

Lenin rejected any attempts, like those by Maxim Gorky, to remake communism into a form of religion. He strongly expressed this view when writing that, "every religious idea, every idea of God, even flirting with the idea of God, is unutterable vileness. ... vileness of the most dangerous kind, 'contagion' of the most abominable kind."[213] Though presented as ideology, Khrushchev's true communism demanded acceptance as a faith and paraded as the substitute for the religions that had embedded in Eastern Europe for many centuries.

The emptiness of communism became more apparent each year. A young Baptist believer in the Moldovan military was brutally murdered for his faith in 1970, and many were still imprisoned or greatly restricted in their freedoms.[214] Printing presses were confiscated, and last-ditch measures were attempted to force all believers into registered churches.[215] These were the attempts of a dying system that no longer had the conviction to pursue its stated goals. The light would overcome the darkness, and the Church would emerge stronger under communism.

## The Berlin Wall

The "Cold War," which started in the 1950s, grew increasingly hotter. Khrushchev (with cooperation from West Germany) decided to separate his empire once and for all by constructing the Berlin Wall in one night, between August 12 and 13, 1961. No longer would East Germany, which became a part of the USSR after WWII, be connected to West Germany, and no longer would intellectual East Germans be able to move to the West. A physical symbol of a closed Eastern Europe stood before the world.

Before and during WWII, a barrier already had been erected that prevented most IMB missionaries from working easily or at all in Eastern Europe. The Berlin Wall was further evidence that the work was closed. Khrushchev was out of power in 1964, and Brezhnev was in to continue communism. Nearly four decades had gone by since a new missionary was appointed to Eastern Europe. But a crack came in the wall in 1976 for the IMB.

# A crack in the wall

James Williams, a Georgia Tech student who was involved in the campus Baptist Student Union and attended First Baptist Church of Atlanta, had an interest in studying overseas as an exchange student. He applied to go to Czechoslovakia but due to unrest there, he had to apply elsewhere. So he applied to go to Yugoslavia and arrived in Zagreb in 1968. Although he was a chemistry major, he also studied the language at the university. Being a Christian, he made it a priority to get involved in ministry at a local Baptist church in Zagreb. The pastor of the church was Josip Horak, who coincidentally was the son-in-law of the late Vincent Vacek, since he had married Vacek's daughter, Elza. (It's a small world for Baptists! As you recall, Vacek was well acquainted with Dr. Gill and was well known for his evangelism in this part of the world.)

The young Williams helped where he could in the church and with English translation for the radio ministry. Horak took Williams under his wing, liking him a lot. The church was where Williams met the pastor's daughter, Nela. Nela was practically fluent in three languages and was able to converse with the young American, plus she also attended the same university where he was an exchange student. As you can guess, another love story between an American and Eastern European! Nela's goal in life was to be a missionary and due to the time he spent being mentored by her father in ministry, Williams's heart turned to missions as well. Williams and Nela fell in love and were married the next year. Their first child, a daughter, came along a couple of years later, and they both attended and graduated from the International Baptist Seminary in Ruschlikon, Switzerland, in 1973. They lived in the States for a brief period so that James could earn his Ph.D. in biblical studies and Nela could become a United States citizen.[216] Following God's call, the Williamses were appointed to serve as residential missionaries in Novi Sad, Yugoslavia, on June 29, 1976.[217] Due to her Yugoslavian birth, their young family of four (a son had been born and was a preschooler) was able to live and serve in the country after appointment in 1976.

For over two years, the Williamses were involved in training others in Christian service at the Baptist Bible school in Novi Sad (now Serbia). They then moved to Zagreb to teach at the Bible college. It was a "moving home" for Nela, since Zagreb was where she grew up and where her parents lived. Her parents would be able to see their grandchildren, two elementary-aged and a newborn boy. Tragically in 1980, the same year that the United States would boycott the Olympic games hosted in Moscow, James Williams was killed in a head-on collision, leaving his young widow to raise three children and face an uncertain future.

Nela was given the option by the IMB to return to her husband's native state of Georgia in the United States, but she remembered the call God gave her for missions. "I was called as a missionary before I met my husband," said Nela. "My call was the crucial factor in making the decision." She chose to remain in Yugoslavia and raise her children as a single missionary, with the help of her parents. She continued to teach Greek at the Bible school in Novi Sad, where she had been traveling to once a month, and also at the Bible college in Zagreb. Seeing the need, she wrote the Greek textbook for her students to use. In case you are wondering, her story isn't over!

> "I was called as a missionary before I met my husband."

Though impossible to have residential missionaries in the country, except for Nela Williams, personnel were able to travel regularly from the West. John David Hopper was appointed to serve in Ruschlikon in 1965 but soon became an ambassador for the IMB to the countries of Eastern Europe. From his base in Switzerland, and for several years in Salzburg, he traveled often into the countries of the East. For several semesters, he traveled monthly, sometimes weekly, to Novi Sad to teach courses at the school.[218]

## Signs of the time

When Brezhnev died in 1982, leaders succeeded, and strangely died quickly. Andropov stepped in for a couple of years until he died; Chernenko came to power and was dead one year later. Gorbachev, with a very visible birthmark on his head that the world took notice of, came to power in 1985. Perestroika and Glasnost policies began the next year.

## The Berlin Wall falls

The wall that had become visible in one night in 1961 finally started to tumble in an event I remember well from television news on November 9, 1989. Protestors from both the East and especially the West could be seen converging to the physical symbol of the Iron Curtain, and Eastern European communism was being shattered right before our eyes. I understood some of the significance of that day, but I didn't see the impact that event had until I arrived in Poland less than a year later to preach at a crusade.

Eastern Europe then became a reality for me.

# 5

## CHALLENGES AFTER THE BERLIN WALL FALLS

He couldn't believe what he was hearing. Jim Smith, an IMB missionary who lived in West Berlin and often traveled into East Germany to meet with believers, sat in his car at "Check Point Charlie" on November 9, 1989, waiting to go back through the Berlin Wall into West Berlin. He had been teaching *MasterLife* for a week at the East German Baptist Theological Seminary in Buckow, only 40 kilometers from Poland. While there, everyone was discussing the protests that were happening on the eastern side of the wall in Leipzig, Dresden, and East Berlin. The week before, 1 million people had rallied in the central square in East Berlin. Relatives of some of the seminary students had been arrested, and the atmosphere was tense for everyone wondering what would happen. Christians on both sides of the wall began spontaneous prayer meetings for freedom to come peacefully. After leaving the seminary in his car to head home, Smith heard the news on the radio.

"It was like an Orson Welles broadcast hoax," said Smith. The news was so incredible that he even changed radio stations several times, hearing both East German radio and West German radio reports. Sitting in his car in the queue to get across the border, he finally picked up the United States Armed Forces Radio

Network that reported the end of an era and that the wall was going to open. When it was Smith's turn to go through the border, he noticed the guards were "nervous and fidgety," unlike their usual arrogant manner. "I was waved through quickly and drove straight home. My wife greeted me at the door, and we immediately became glued to the television to see history unfolding as my young children slept peacefully in their beds. We stayed up until 3 a.m. to watch the reports of crowds on both sides gathering at two or three of the border crossings at the [Berlin] Wall. My wife and I couldn't believe it and how fast it was happening," said Smith. At the Brandenburg Gate, students had used ladders to climb on the part that was 10-feet thick and flat, and by early morning November 10, Smith's birthday, East German soldiers were blasting water hoses to force them down. The masses at the wall had heard the official statement aired on the radio that announced the wall would open for people of the East to travel to the West. Years later, it came to light that the communist official actually misread the statement and mistakenly announced open travel versus a more carefully crafted statement requiring more of a process to open the border. There was no way the announcement could be revoked, and history was forever changed.

On the 10th, people on the western side began chipping away at the wall. There were fears that people would be shot by the East German soldiers standing on top, but nothing happened. In fact, no one was ever shot. "That was miraculous," commented Smith. "It was God's protection that the communists would cave in to a nonviolent, peaceful protest."

That night, Smith drove to the western side of the wall and parked as close as he could. "It was crazy," he said. "Every kind of person was there. They were bringing hammers and hacksaws and metal tools to attack the [Berlin] Wall. With the music and crowds, it was like a rock concert atmosphere." (He confessed that he had suitcases full of chunks of the wall that he kept after his family made several outings to help break it down. They gave pieces as gifts for years!) By November 11, international media personnel were everywhere, and Smith said that with all the influx of people pouring in from East Germany, hotels were packed. He had Baptist Press journalists sleeping on the floor of their apartment, and secular journalists contacted him for interviews. "Our house was Grand Central Station for the next six months! We remember this time fondly, but we were tired!" admitted Smith. "It was a whirlwind."

Rather emotional as he reflected on that time in history, Smith added, "During the day on November 9 (before any radio announcement was made), my 5-year-old daughter went to my wife and asked, 'Is Daddy going to be home for his birthday?' which was the next day, November 10. My wife explained to her that she hoped so, but that I was still on the other side of the wall and hadn't gotten through yet. 'Well,' she replied, 'I'm going to pray tonight that God will tear down that wall!' So she did. I made it through the border and home on one of the most famous nights of the century. That night changed our whole lives. And I was home for my birthday, just as my little girl prayed."[219]

## Anticipating the new era before the fall

The end of the 1980s welcomed a time of global upheaval largely due to the changes of the Soviet Union. The IMB had been preparing itself for the unknown time when the USSR would dissolve. After the 1976 appointment of the Williamses, the first IMB missionaries in Eastern Europe in a long time, the IMB opened up an office in 1983 for the East Europe Mission in Vienna, Austria, anticipating that more residential missionaries would follow.[220] Other than Nela Williams, unexpectedly single and born in Yugoslavia, no one from the IMB could secure a residency permit behind the Iron Curtain, so missionaries, like Jim and Becky Smith in West Berlin, traveled in as tourists to work.

Missionaries were also meeting Eastern Europeans at the seminary in Ruschlikon. Occasionally, students from the Soviet Union were granted permission to study there. This was a major hub for the IMB to connect and network with the leaders from the Eastern Bloc countries. The seminary began a lay institute on its campus in 1988 under the leadership of Earl Martin.[221] By this time, more Eastern European participants were able to attend.

An important development in 1988, a year before the Berlin Wall fell, was the "70/30 Plan."[222] IMB President Keith Parks wrote, "The 10-year plan to have 70 percent of Southern Baptist missionaries giving more than half of their time to evangelistic outreach and church planting is part of the Southern Baptist International Mission Board's effort to escalate the rate of reaching the world for Christ."[223] This measure was passed by IMB trustees and would be implemented during the arrival of the first missionaries in the former Soviet Union.

## Religious freedom returns

After the East was opened to the West during 1989 and 1990, all the hideous things that had happened under communism were revealed in the years that followed. Freedom came in many forms. The oppressed people under communism were thrust into the secularism of the West. Instead of people turning to God, many defined hope as buying things that had been unavailable to them in their bleak economies, visiting other countries, or moving out of Eastern Europe completely. Even Christians fled, leaving a big gap for Christian growth in the East. People were seduced by the West, according to Jim Smith. "Churches were at their fullest before the [Berlin] Wall fell, but that dropped to nothing after protests ended, and people were able to travel without fear of informants or an oppressive government," he said. "[The fall of the wall] was like a tectonic plate had shifted, and our focus was how we were going to get missionaries into Eastern European countries. We had to rethink our whole future."[224]

> "[The fall of the wall] was like a tectonic plate had shifted ..."

As the IMB was rethinking its future in Eastern Europe, some dormant feelings and convictions by Roman Catholicism and Eastern Orthodoxy were reawakened as well. It led to their strong reassertion of status and power.

This Europe was different than pre-WWI. Entering the era of communism, the two traditional churches enjoyed favored status in virtually all of the Central and Eastern European countries but emerged from the communist era with various degrees of status and influence. The Roman Catholic Church of Central Europe and the Orthodox Church of Eastern Europe emerged weaker but, in many ways, were more determined to recover lost ground. Pope John Paul II often called a continent growing in secularism back to the historic faith.[225] Jose Casanova, professor of sociology at Georgetown University, wrote that Western Europe was irreversibly secular.[226] The central and eastern countries in Europe emerged from decades of communism hoping for a quick reintegration with the western region of the continent. Some in these lands feared an inevitable process of secularism as the countries of Europe reunited.

Pope John Paul II encouraged the Catholic Church of Poland to embrace European integration as "a great apostolic assignment."[227] The Polish Episcopate energetically accepted the Pope's assignment and underscored one of its chief goals "to restore Europe for Christianity."[228] Many Poles saw historic precedent for this central role in strengthening the Church. The reassertion of traditional churches of the West and East coupled with an unabated rise of secularism and the recent rise of Islam combined to create a new Europe with many questions and uncertainties.

In 1990, Muslims were a majority population in Albania (80 percent) and Kosovo (85 percent) and had substantial minorities in Bosnia and Herzegovina (44 percent), Macedonia (30 percent), and Montenegro (21 percent).[229] They also numbered over 12 million in Russia, comprising about 8 percent of the population.[230] Braswell recorded that about 70 percent of the people in Albania professed Islam when the communists seized power in 1944.[231] In 1967, religion was abolished there and in 1976, the constitution prohibited all religious organizations.[232] These restrictions were removed when the communist government fell in 1991. Substantial Muslim populations existed in Yugoslavia among Albanians, Macedonians, Montenegrins, Kosovars, Bosnians, and Turks. The communist government of Yugoslavia gave

Muslims a national status in 1988, which led to polarization and heightened aspirations.[233] The clash of these aspirations with new freedoms and nationalistic designs of other ethnic populations in Yugoslavia exploded into several wars in the 1990s.

Though not on the scale of Roman Catholicism or Eastern Orthodoxy, Islam greatly influenced several European countries and provided the context for the work of several missionaries in the early 1990s. Though the practice of Islam was often considered nominal in southern Europe compared to the Middle Eastern expression, it had (and still has) a strong cultural hold over its populations and constituted a real barrier in spreading the gospel and planting churches. The growing missionary activity of Middle Eastern Muslims combined with a high birth rate contributed to the increase of practicing Muslims.

Arguably the most important event on the religious calendar of 1988 was the millennium celebration of the Orthodox Church in Russia. That year signaled 1,000 years since the baptism of Prince Vladimir of Kiev and the official adoption of Christianity.[234] Orthodox leaders presented the celebrations as a way to enrich the spiritual life of the country, encourage greater morality, and raise questions about the meaning of life. Vladimir Sorokin, rector of the Alexander Nevsky Lavra Orthodox Theological Academy and Seminary in Leningrad (now St. Petersburg) wrote, "God helps us make people think about what we lost when we destroyed our churches. Our society lost its soul."[235]

President Gorbachev saw the rapid decline of the Soviet Union and sought to strengthen it through a greater openness. He met with the Orthodox Patriarch Pimen and agreed to sweeping reforms and the reopening of thousands of Orthodox churches.[236] This was a big step in the subsequent reopening of evangelical churches. More than 1,700 Orthodox religious societies or parishes were registered in 1988 and 1989.[237] The place of favored status was again being secured and strengthened with the fall of the communist government.

## Making the most of the opportunity

The increasing decline of the Soviet Union raised the hopes of the IMB, and the increased contact with church leaders prompted greater partnership and monetary investment in the work. IMB leaders traveled to much of the region in 1988 and 1989 and compiled a list of capital needs for work in seven of the countries: Czechoslovakia, Poland, Hungary, Yugoslavia, East Germany, Bulgaria, and the USSR.[238] The list included medical equipment, construction assistance for churches, training centers and camps, printing presses, computers, and other ministry-related items.[239] Multiple countries were entered in 1990 for the first time by IMB residential missionaries.

Keith Parks had issued an intensive response for the IMB in Eastern Europe, which was later termed a "Green Alert." The initiative specifically called for a task force to be assembled, comprised of Lewis Myers (vice president, Cooperative Services International), Keith Parker (Area Director, Europe), Paul Thibodeaux (associate to the area director, Europe), Mike Stroope (field base coordinator for Cooperative Services International), Brian Grim (representative of Cooperative Services International), Jim Smith (Eastern Europe Partnership Mission coordinator and representative to the Baltic states), George Lozuk (missionary, USSR), and Isam Ballenger (vice president, Europe, Middle East, and North Africa and chairman of the task force).[240] The purpose of the task force was to figure out a strategy for this newly opened region.[241]

The Green Alert proposal had three key areas that were developed into action plans, deployment goals, and budget requests. Paraphrased, these three major divisions were to strengthen local Baptists in their effort to evangelize their lands through training; provide Christian witness to the unreached/unevangelized peoples and help facilitate appropriate structures for their worship and training, particularly by cooperating with other groups to make the Bible and the *JESUS* film available in every major language of the former Soviet Union; and send career and short-term missionaries and volunteers.[242]

61

Not long after this proposal, requests were made for 50 career units, 157 ISC workers, vast numbers of volunteers, and over $4 million for the work in the Central Asian republics of the former Soviet Union.[243] It went further in requesting 89 career missionaries, 189 ISC workers, at least 1,289 volunteers, and $8 million for the work in Eastern Europe.[244] Such numbers were unprecedented in the history of the IMB.

As things go, following the visionary report by the task force, the trustees turned their attention to the defunding of the International Baptist Theological Seminary in Ruschlikon.[245] This discussion led to controversy and heated exchange with the seminary and also led to a split between the IMB and the European Baptist Federation (EBF), as well as many Baptist unions. Several IMB missionaries in Europe resigned in protest of this decision.[246] The controversy also diverted attention and momentum from the new opportunities in Eastern Europe toward the defense of the decision. The proposals for advance so heartily approved were never fully implemented, and entrance into these newly opened lands took much longer than expected.

## The task ahead

Keith Parks returned from a trip to Budapest in 1989 where the great needs of Eastern Europe were discussed with various union leaders, and he returned to Richmond full of hope for the new day. But three years later, Parks would not be a part of the IMB's initiative into Eastern Europe. Under a cloud of controversy between trustees and him, Parks gave his resignation effective October 30, 1992.[247] He later reflected that this distraction from the open door in Eastern Europe was one of his greatest regrets.[248] Jerry Rankin, who had served many years in Asia, became the next IMB president.

A significant development in 1992 was the naming of Sam James to step into the role vacated by the resignation of Isam Ballenger. After 30 years of service in Asia, James agreed to serve as the IMB regional vice president for Europe, the Middle East, and North Africa, as well as assume the role of interim area director for Europe.[249] Even the EBF leaders agreed that James was the perfect choice for this role of reconciliation at that critical juncture.[250]

James was given the nearly impossible task of addressing the deep concerns of European leaders, supporting the recent actions of the IMB Board of Trustees, and fully seizing new opportunities in Eastern Europe. He wrote of the scene that welcomed him to his new position following the defunding of the International Baptist Theological Seminary in Ruschlikon:

> *The result was that the European Baptist Federation and almost every Baptist union in Western Europe broke relations with the IMB. All the regional leadership staff except for three associates resigned almost immediately. Two of these associates resigned within a few months. Thirty-three missionaries resigned and many more were on the verge of resigning. The European Baptist Federation leadership refused to entertain the senior vice president for overseas operation of the IMB when he asked to visit.*[251]

Soon after James' appointment, the EBF extended him an invitation to attend a special meeting in Hamburg, Germany. Along with two trustees, Skip Smith and Bill Blanchard, and the IMB executive vice president, Don Kammerdiener, James attended this historic meeting in September, 1992.[252]

"Bristling with hostility and tension" was the atmosphere. During the first day and a half, the Europeans pushed hard for an apology, and the trustees pushed for a resolution. Finally, the trustees mentioned some points in the recent process, which opened the door for some frank, yet constructive dialogue. The meeting ended with the "Hamburg Agreement," which addressed the inherent need for real discussions and consultation before reaching important decisions that affected the work in Europe.[253]

Following the Hamburg meeting, James and other leaders began reengaging with the union leaders in Eastern Europe. Though not as emotionally involved in the controversy as the western union leaders, some union officers in the former Soviet Union watched the process with interest. James described the early IMB strategy in Eastern Europe as:

> *To invest in nationals with capability to serve rather than short-term projects or buildings. Discipleship training, pastor training, lay training were the identified long-term needs, which the IMB could provide with its limited resources. Assisting pastors with a vision for planting churches and working with those pastors in church planting was a central part of the immediate IMB strategy.*[254]

But what about the Southern Baptists in the United States? They were flooding into Eastern Europe when the area opened up. Though well-meaning, many immediately began sponsoring pastors and subsidizing programs and buildings, which prompted unhealthy dependence.[255] This prompted the early decision by the IMB to assign volunteer coordinators to most of the countries emerging from the Soviet Union.

It is important to note that though church planters were listed on the priority list for new personnel, few of the first wave of missionaries carried the title of church planter, and most did not see this as the priority of their assignment. Even those with the title of church planter were often directed to the along-side role of encouraging nationals to plant churches. The position described as "liaison personnel," and later defined as "fraternal representative," became the entrance assignment as new countries were opened.

After the initial transfers settled into their fraternal representative roles, they began to consult with union leaders about job requests for new IMB personnel. Some job requests still existed from the earlier consultations between Jim Smith, Paul Thibodeaux, and union leaders, but many new ones were submitted.[256] The policy of the IMB until the late 1990s was that personnel would not be deployed to a country with a Baptist Union unless that Union signed off on the job request.[257] This necessity slowed the process of deploying new missionaries into Eastern Europe.

The new job requests written in the early 1990s included theological educators and church developers, but the majority of the new jobs in Eastern Europe were for church planters to plant indigenous churches.[258] This new emphasis of church planting by the new IMB president was warmly embraced and furthered by John Floyd, the newly elected area director for Europe in 1993.[259] In his report to trustees the following year, he underscored: "The potential requests for Eastern Europe are almost unlimited. There is an urgent need for 100 church-planting and church-developing missionaries immediately in Eastern Europe. Several countries need to be entered, and other countries need strengthening in the numbers of personnel."[260] Many new missionaries responded to the call in the former Soviet Union, and the first wave of new appointees began to grow by the middle of the decade. The majority of initial IMB-founded churches resulted from these missionaries appointed in the 1990s.

> Many new missionaries responded to the call in the former Soviet Union, and the first wave of new appointees began to grow by the middle of the decade.

Another crucial development in the IMB under Rankin's leadership was a restructuring called "New Directions."[261] The structure centered around 14 regions, which were led by an on-site regional leader. Avery Willis, IMB senior vice president for overseas operations, commented:

> As we began to look again at what God is saying to us, we saw there were some things we needed to come back to. "New Directions" is a return to a biblical mandate. The Bible is what we want our missionary manual to be. The basic concepts of New Directions are: 1) A strong emphasis on prayer support; 2) focusing on people groups wherever they are instead of organizing by countries; 3) missionaries who work in teams to plan comprehensive strategies for sharing the gospel with entire people groups; 4) lay training programs that enable new believers to move quickly into church leadership roles; 5) working in cooperation with "Great Commission Christian" mission partners; 6) working and praying for God-led, church-

*planting movements to begin; and 7) a general "whatever it takes" approach to sharing the gospel, despite social, political, cultural, or other barriers.*[262]

By the end of the decade, these new measures were often interpreted by EEU leaders as a step toward independent service in their countries. The IMB missionaries had to over communicate the continued desire to work in partnership with national Baptist unions and accelerate the church planting that was going on in each country.

The title of fraternal representative was used widely for the first personnel who came into Eastern Europe after 1989, but that changed as well as strategies in the new millennium. Missionary training and strategy became even more culturally sensitive, and cooperation with national and United States church partners became even more important as relationships grew.

An important general development at the end of the century was the rise of intentional church planting among people groups and immigrant populations in Europe.[263] One of these people groups was the Roma, or Gypsies, found in Romania, Poland, Macedonia, Slovakia, Bulgaria, and the Czech Republic.[264]

In 1999, John Floyd retired as the regional leader and was replaced by Rodney Hammer, who continued to give visionary leadership to the region. Hundreds of missionaries arrived in the new millennium for service in the newly formed Central and Eastern Europe region of the IMB. And after Hammer's leadership, I currently am leading IMB work with all European peoples, now called an "affinity" instead of region due to our present focus on people groups. After Rankin's retirement in July 2011, Tom Elliff became the IMB president.

Having given the background of how quickly things changed beginning in 1989 for evangelical efforts, particularly what it meant for the IMB, it's time to have a detailed look at the work of God after this "break in the wall." When everything opened back up in Eastern Europe, we hadn't yet put the focus on people groups instead of countries. For simplicity, since we already looked at where missionaries like

Dr. and Mrs. Gill and others worked before the Berlin Wall fell, you'll get a better picture of what has happened since 1989 in Eastern Europe if we go country by country. Even the boundaries and names of countries have changed.

By the way, in the chapters remaining, missionary, worker, and personnel will be used interchangeably. The IMB refers to missionaries as "workers" these days. Out of the many IMB workers who have come in the last 20 years, I'll mention the fascinating stories of some.

# YUGOSLAVIA

*(Croatia, Serbia, Montenegro, Slovenia, Bosnia and Herzegovina, Kosovo, and Macedonia)*

Admit it. You've been wondering what happened to Nela Williams.

When Nela was growing up in Yugoslavia, many diverse ethnic groups were forced together into that country and were ruled with a strong hand during the communist era. In the early 1990s, the breakup of the Soviet Union and fall of communist rule prompted the disintegration of Yugoslavia into five separate countries by the end of the last century.[265]

Let's go back earlier than Nela and even before communism became a force. Remember Vincent Vacek? I haven't completely filled you in on his story. When Vacek, an immigrant from Yugoslavia, heard the gospel preached by a street preacher in Detroit, Michigan, at the beginning of the 20th century, he responded with faith. He returned to Yugoslavia with his wife and seven children (one being Elza) to share this newfound faith as a pastor and evangelist.[266] He founded the Baptist Union of Yugoslavia and became a missionary to his own people. He also began to receive support from the IMB in 1923 as he concentrated on evangelism, as earlier mentioned, and started churches throughout the country.[267] His daughter, Elza, married Josip Horak, who became a pastor and the Baptist Union leader and served faithfully until his death in 1999.[268] Horak also served as a vice president of the Baptist World Alliance.[269]

Horak's daughter, and Vacek's granddaughter, was named Nela. Our Nela. "My father was a pastor," said Nela, "so I was prepared to respond to the call to full-time missions while still a teenager."[270] As you know, she married an American exchange student in Zagreb, James Williams, and they pursued that call to missions together to Eastern Europe in 1976 as the only IMB residential missionaries in Eastern Europe sent between 1941 and 1988. James was killed in a tragic car accident in 1980, but Nela, along with her three young children, continued her faithful service in Yugoslavia, despite the challenges. So that's a summary to get you prepared for her continuing story. Hang on.

In 1988, eight years after the death of Nela's husband, a nontourist visa was approved for new IMB colleagues for the first time in Eastern Europe in nearly 50 years.[271] Nela finally would have some IMB personnel join her. It was fitting that one of the last countries evacuated by IMB personnel at the outbreak of World War II was the first country re-entered as the Soviet Union began to rapidly decline in the late 1980s.

## New personnel and a disappearing Yugoslavia

Bill and Debbie Steele were appointed by the IMB in 1988 and arrived in Yugoslavia later that year.[272] They entered on student visas and studied the language for two years before applying and receiving religious visas in 1990. That same year, they were given the title of fraternal representative to Yugoslavia and began relating more fully to the Baptist Union. For the first five years, they made their home in Belgrade and worked closely with the Union leadership. Steele described their initial years as "communist with spiraling inflation and pre-fall wall mentality."[273] He also confirmed, "We had a good relationship with the national leaders in Yugoslavia during these years."[274]

The break-up of Yugoslavia was not peaceful and prompted various wars that lasted throughout the 1990s. Before I go any further, let me introduce current names for the break-up that I will interchange with former Yugoslavia. Eventually the big country of Yugoslavia was divided into several geographical countries or political unions. Not to go into the differences, for our purposes I'll give the names and the years independence was formally declared: Slovenia (1991), Croatia (1991), Bosnia and Herzegovina (1992), and Serbia and Montenegro (2006). Part of Macedonia had been in Yugoslavia as well.

Steele wrote that the outbreak of hostilities in 1992 completely changed the complexion of their work. He asserted, "I spent an inordinate amount of time working with the Union-sponsored humanitarian organizations for Bosnia, Croatia, Slovenia, and Serbia during the War years from 1992 to 1997. I worked under the umbrella of an NGO that I formed in Bosnia from 1997 to 1999."[275] Unfortunately, the overwhelming need for humanitarian assistance overshadowed other priorities, like evangelism and church planting, during the first half of the decade. The flow of amazing sums of money through the churches brought an unhealthy dependence upon Western sources of support.

The Steeles relocated several times in their 12 years of service. They based in Belgrade until 1992 when they moved to Ljubljana, Slovenia, from 1993 to 1995. They moved to Split, Croatia, from 1995 to 1996 and finished their service with the IMB in Sarajevo, Bosnia, from 1996 to 1999.[276]

Toward the end of their second term, when the Steeles moved to the coastal town of Split, they participated directly in church planting. Though the plague of military skirmishes did not disappear, they were able to invest in some local believers and leaders to help establish a new Baptist church in 1995. The church started with 15 members and soon selected a pastor to lead them in a rented, public building. Steele was able to coach the new pastor and assist him for 13 months in the solidification of the new church. The church continued to grow slowly and remains vibrant 15 years later.[277]

The Steeles faced many challenges regarding ethical dilemmas and various cultural practices. They were confronted with issues like smuggling Bibles and audio-video equipment past customs agents or paying bribes in order to release urgently needed materials. Even simple tasks like exchanging American currency presented problems, because the official government offices and standard rates were drastically lower than the black market exchange on the streets. Being first-term missionaries and not transfers, they entered an uncharted context for the IMB. The expectations of their assignment changed drastically, and annually, due to the reality of the Balkan Peninsula and the continued ethnic hostilities within Yugoslavia. The ongoing strife not only led to ever-changing assignments but also prompted many moves for the family. By their third term, the Steeles were learning to balance the constant demands for humanitarian aid, Union requests for funding, and the priority need of planting churches.[278]

In 1994, Randy and Joan Bell arrived in Belgrade and began working in the Serbian part of Yugoslavia while the war involving Serbs, Croats, and Bosnians was still going strong. They received humanitarian aid visas and worked closely with refugees in the regions of Serbia and Bosnia. By 1996, under the supervision of Bill Steele, the Bells began to partner with national Baptists in the establishment of several Bible studies and fledgling churches.[279]

They reported the start of new groups in New Belgrade, Bijelo Polje, Montenegro, Loznica, Banja Luka, Sarajevo, and Prijedor over a four-year period (1996–1999).[280] At the same time, John Floyd, area director for Europe, put out a call for six couples to relocate and seize the open opportunity in the disintegrating country of Yugoslavia.[281] By October 1996, four veteran IMB couples had agreed to move and serve a term: the Worleys from Spain; the Leepers from Germany; the Fredericks from France; and the Millers, who were recently retired from the Philippines.[282] Two other couples later made similar commitments for two to three years.[283]

In October 1996, Floyd described the start of new work in the Bosnian city of Tuzla. It was the place where soldiers were building a bridge and a place where so many IMB interests were. Aid had been going into Tuzla, and nationals were starting to notice. "These folks (IMB missionaries) went into ... Tuzla where they had been distributing food packets and humanitarian relief and had a three-day meeting in a hotel. Over 100 people made professions of faith." The Fredericks and Leepers followed up with these and many others who had received food packets and who indicated a desire for Bible study. They discovered that 208 were interested for them to start Bible studies. Not only that, worship services started, and the response was enormous. They worked with ministry partners and interpreters.[284] Todd and Kim Golden arrived in Bosnia in 1997 and served as strategy coordinators until 2008. They were instrumental in the publication of the Bosnian New Testament and extensively used volunteers to pass out tens of thousands of copies to a total of 200,000 Bosnians. Among the many key partners was the Woman's Missionary Union. Despite the war and uncertainty, over 100 WMU volunteers participated in projects from 1997 to 2000.

> They discovered that 208 were interested for them to start Bible studies. Not only that, worship services started, and the response was enormous.

Trey and Elise Atkins arrived in 1999 to continue casting the vision for new churches in Bosnia.[285] They saw a couple of new groups form, but these did not survive past the initial two to three years. They influenced the existing church in Sarajevo to begin an outreach ministry among children, youth, and college students, and these efforts saw some fruit.[286]

By the mid-1990s, Richard and Beverly Bell arrived in Zapresic, near Zagreb, to assist the fledgling work in Croatia. Richard was a trained veterinarian but focused on encouraging the small group of believers and training in discipleship.

Kyle and Jackie Kirkpatrick were appointed in 1996 and opened the work in the newly formed country of Macedonia.[287] The nation broke away from Yugoslavia in the early 1990s and largely avoided the decade of wars on the Balkan Peninsula. Kirkpatrick described the setting upon their arrival: "The country was dominated by the Orthodox Church. Protestants had some old-line churches that had survived communism but were fairly beaten down and with a fortress mentality. The Baptist

Union had two churches, and one was dying. "[288] The Kirkpatricks worked closely with the existing churches during language study and encouraged a vision for church planting. They were also instrumental in assisting with some construction and literature projects.

In 1998, a group left the existing church in Skopje, which prompted the first attempt at starting a new work. The Kirkpatricks helped to make the most of an unfortunate situation and instilled sound principles in church planting. The splinter group emerged as a new church. A new step was taken related to evangelism among the Roma and the start of some small groups. Most of the new groups did not really mature but work among the Roma increased and became independent of the mother church. The work of the Kirkpatricks continued into the new century.

Recently, the Baptist Union in Macedonia and IMB personnel together have initiated work in Ohrid and Prilep. IMB workers have transferred from Skopje to Prilep, and new workers have been deployed to Ohrid.

As you've noticed the name changes (and you might want to Google maps of Yugoslavia and the breakup of Yugoslavia), the IMB work in Yugoslavia divided as the country became multiple countries. Personnel appointments increased into every emerging country and presently serve in Serbia, Croatia, Slovenia, Bosnia and Herzegovina, Macedonia, Kosovo, and Montenegro. Some of the workers from the 1990s continue to serve in these countries, focusing on people groups rather than borders, and now give leadership to much of the work.

In 1999, IMB workers were forced to evacuate Serbia due to bombing by United States troops.[289] Randy and Joan Bell relocated to Maribor, Slovenia. Slovenia withdrew from Yugoslavia in 1991 and after a brief skirmish, secured independence.[290] The Bells immediately began language study and connected with the small Baptist Union. After a year, they cooperated with Baptist leaders in establishing groups in Murska Sobota and Maribor. The first group met for about a year but discontinued after strife emerged among the leaders.[291]

In 2001, a special evangelistic event was scheduled in Maribor. Cooperating with Campus Crusade and the two evangelical churches in town, the Bells helped plan and conduct an outreach using the *JESUS* film. Over 2,500 individuals came. Over 100 viewers filled out an interest form, and the two churches, along with the Bells, divided up these cards. The Bells followed up with 35 names given to them and invited each family to a new Bible study set to begin in their home in January 2002. Two people, Martin and Ilika, showed up to the first Bible study, and both soon came to faith and were the foundation for starting the new church.[292] Even as the new church grew, it saw the need to start a new church in Slovenj Gradec, located about an hour west of Maribor. The group there continued to grow steadily and became a recognized church within a few years.

National partners generally led these new churches in Slovenia, and IMB personnel provided training and coaching for them. The small Union more than doubled in its first decade and continues to slowly target new towns and villages. About half of the groups started in the late 1990s still functioned as autonomous churches a decade later.[293]

One of the greatest evangelistic weeks in the history of Slovenia occurred in 2011 when a coordinated effort of evangelicals brought Nick Vujicic, author of *Without Limits* and an evangelist from Australia, to speak in five cities, two where no evangelical churches existed. Over 17,000 people heard the gospel in these cities. Never had this many Slovenians heard the gospel at once. The Bells coordinated the event in Maribor, which 3,500 people attended. New Bible study groups have started all over the country as a result.

Work in Croatia was re-established in the 1990s, but the first strong groups emerged after 2000. Currently groups have been formed in Zagreb and Split.[294] Trey and Elise Atkins in Zagreb and Eric and Julie Maroney in Split have been catalytic in these young churches. Similarly, new groups have been started in Cacak and Kraljevo, Serbia.[295] IMB workers entered Kosovo after the hostilities with Serbia subsided in 2000, and the first workers were deployed into Montenegro in 2008.[296] Fledgling groups have been established in these places.

Finally, back to Nela. Once the civil war in the broken-up Yugoslavia began in earnest, Nela could not travel to the seminary in Novi Sad (since it had become Serbia), but she continued to teach and minister in Zagreb (which became Croatia). By this time, her two oldest children were in the States at universities. Between 1992 and 1994, the war was so intense that Nela sent her youngest son to live with his Grandmother and Grandfather Williams in the States to complete seventh and eighth grades. "That was the worst part of the war," she said. After she came to the States on furlough to see her children and in-laws, she returned with him to Croatia in 1994, where she continued to minister.

After nearly 35 years, Nela Williams retired from the IMB in May 2011. She raised three children by herself (all married now and work in the States) and had a fruitful ministry for the Lord in Yugoslavia/Croatia as a widow. (It would be a good time to get out a tissue!) Two years before retirement, one of her Swiss friends died. She had known this woman and her husband, Peter Mayer, for about 25 years since she had met them in Switzerland, where she was occasionally a guest. The Mayers had been former missionaries to Portugal and Central Asia. When Peter's wife died in 2009, Nela sent him a letter of condolence. She knew what he must be going through to lose his beloved spouse, for Nela herself had been a widow for nearly 30 years. Peter wrote her back, which began regular letter exchanges. Another love story developed. "So it was very beautiful," said Nela, concerning what happened between them late in life. They married in June 2011, one month after Nela's retirement from the IMB and now live and serve faithfully in Zagreb, Croatia, when they are not visiting children and grandchildren. They use English to converse, since that is their common language, although not either of their heart languages. "But he is learning Croatian now!" announced Nela. Nela has truly lived through changes in her personal life, the country of her birth, and her God-called ministry, but she has never given up serving God and the people in Eastern Europe.[297]

# 7

## HUNGARY

The seminary in Ruschlikon began to develop a lay academy in 1988 under the umbrella of their Institute for Evangelism and Missions. The same year, it was determined that the long-term location of this training program, called International Baptist Lay Academy (IBLA), would be in Budapest, Hungary.[298] IMB leadership began searching for the appropriate leader for the new training center and tapped Errol Simmons, who along with his wife, Mary, had served many years in Spain.[299] He was chosen by Keith Parker, area director at that time, because Simmons was a veteran missionary with grown children who had an earned a doctorate and experience as a theological educator.[300] The Simmonses moved to Budapest in January 1989 as only the second family to secure a residential visa in Eastern Europe. IBLA began its first courses in the summer of 1990 in the new facility of the Hungarian Baptist Seminary. The objective was to offer training for lay church leaders. Applications from Eastern European church leaders exceeded space for students.[301]

Simmons's main assignment was that of theological training, but he also served as fraternal representative to Hungary and for a year, Czechoslovakia. The work in the latter country was opened the following year by another transfer family, the Fords, who assumed the fraternal representative role at that time. The lay institute was a popular, attractive program for Eastern Europeans to learn English while receiving some basic training in theology. Simmons gave strong leadership to the program and utilized volunteer teachers to help with numerous modules. The lay course lasted one year, which made it fairly easy for students to attend the course and return to their previous employment or studies. During IBLA's decade in Budapest, over 500 students attended from 22 countries.[302] Many of these students went on to hold leadership positions in their national Baptist unions.

In early conversations with IMB leadership, the Hungarian Union leaders spoke cautiously of personnel and wanted a high degree of control of any workers who were sent. Isam Ballenger, regional vice president for Europe, North Africa, and the Middle East, met with the leaders and concluded that "Hungary wanted to stipulate where a missionary would serve, and their preference was not church planting."[303] This approach was the norm for the vast majority of Baptist union leaders in Eastern Europe at this time.

In the final days of the Soviet Union, Hungary was known as one of the most open or lenient communist governments. Simmons recalled that the first European Baptist Federation Congress held in Eastern Europe was in Budapest in 1989. The congress closed with a Billy Graham Crusade; over 50,000 people attended the stadium services with a capacity of 35,000.[304] The overflow crowd stood on the field throughout the service. Simmons served on the crusade committee, and counseling material was prepared for 4,000. At the gospel invitation, over 17,000 responded, which prompted a great season of evangelism for Baptists.[305] This event served as an immense encouragement for the Union to transition out of the shadow of communism.

The Simmonses were joined by the Bodenheimers in March of 1991 and the Jordans in June of the same year. The Bodenheimers served a three-year term before resigning from the IMB, and the Jordans served for three terms, concentrating in the areas of discipleship and church development. In 1992, Steve and Susan Booth were appointed to serve in Budapest, and Steve answered the priority assignment of seminary professor. They worked diligently to learn a challenging language and began to teach a light load of classes at the Baptist seminary. They served two terms before transferring to the Canadian Southern Baptist Seminary in Cochrane, Canada, where they still faithfully serve. Looking back at the time period, Booth summarized the perspective of the Hungarian Baptists as first trying to strengthen their current churches and ministries. They had a shortage of pastors after communism, so they didn't feel like they could start new churches.[306]

It was also a time volunteers poured into Hungary from Southern Baptist churches, which often led to the building of new church buildings or camps and the renovation of existing structures. Many of these volunteers came in conjunction with Baptist state partnerships.[307] Over the course of several years, hundreds of volunteers and thousands of dollars poured into the work of Hungarian Baptists.

The early relationship between IMB personnel and Hungarian Baptists was positive, and IMB workers generally concentrated on the priorities set by the Union. Financial support was requested and received for many years to help with capital projects, but the strategic influence of the missionaries was limited.[308] The Union did not often seek the input of IMB workers related to the starting of new congregations. The Union strongly supported the formal partnership with the Baptist General Convention of Virginia. This relationship lasted from 1991 to 1994, with many teams coming from Virginia churches.[309]

Another desire of the Union was the establishment of an international church. Lewis and Adeline Krause arrived in 1991 and started an English-language international church. The group attracted expatriates from many different countries and a few English-speaking Hungarians. Within a year, the church averaged over 50 in attendance, and, within five years, virtually every country in Eastern Europe had an international Baptist church.[310]

None of the first wave of IMB workers concentrated on the planting of new Hungarian churches. IMB personnel in Hungary, and much of Eastern Europe, had significant turnover during the first 10 to 15 years of the new freedoms. The Simmonses concluded their missionary service in 2000, and, in the same year, IBLA relocated to the International Baptist Theological Seminary that moved from Ruschlikon to Prague.[311]

Most of the work in Hungary in the latter 1990s continued in the areas of church development and theological education. The Jordans continued to assist with Sunday school teacher training and discipleship workshops, especially near their home in Szeged. Steve Booth continued to teach New Testament at the Hungarian Baptist Theological Seminary in Budapest.[312] Ron and Robin Brown arrived and after language study in Szeged, deployed to start a group in Gyor.[313]

Though workers re-entered Hungary in 1989, it took more than a decade before a meaningful church-planting influence developed. Mark and Kristie Aderholt arrived in Budapest in 2000 and began learning Hungarian.[314] They also began casting a vision for church planting that would reproduce more churches. Their team led church-planting movement workshops.[315] One of the attendees at several of these workshops was Durko Istvan, associate pastor of a church and director of the student division of the Baptist Union. He was an "insider."[316] Aderholt was able to mentor Istvan and, along with four core families, encouraged him in a church start in 2003. The decision was made to launch the church in Budaors, which was a suburb just west of Budapest. Many new apartment buildings, industrial parks, shopping centers, and other establishments were being built in this suburb.

In January 2003, the planting team met with leaders of existing churches to seek their blessing and alleviate unnecessary suspicions of competition. The blessing was given and weekly meetings began, both in homes and in a rented school building.[317] The new work slowly began to grow through constant promotion, community events, and outreach projects. Contact among students especially proved fruitful. By the beginning of the third year in 2005, the church had grown to a membership of over 50 and, more importantly, had developed a vision for starting additional groups and churches in the city and beyond.[318]

Since then groups have emerged in Nagykanizsa, Gyor, Debrecen, and Budapest. Much of the growth has been among students in these cities, and baptisms have become more commonplace after many years of faithful, gospel sowing. Some new believers are now being trained to start new outreach groups.[319]

# ROMANIA

After a long absence, the IMB's work resumed in Romania in June 1991 with the arrival of T. and Kathie Thomas and their youngest three daughters.[320] They had served in France for 13 years and transferred to a nation in turmoil and great transition. During their last year in Paris, the Thomases began studying Romanian, and T. was able to take four trips there to meet leadership and assess the situation.

T. was embraced by the Union leadership and offered office space in their building, which the IMB had purchased for the Union years ago.[321] As they unpacked their belongings, they discovered an economy in shambles with empty grocery stores. He asserted that the generosity of believers and food from the countryside sustained them through the first winter. He also remembered that the churches were filled to overflowing. People were standing in every open space of the chapel, and often even more people were outside trying to listen through the open windows. Sunday mornings at church usually began with an hour of spontaneous prayer, followed by an hour of Sunday school, and then a two-hour worship service with multiple sermons.[322] People were spiritually hungry.

Thomas was immediately asked to teach evangelism and missions at the seminary. The communist government had previously capped enrollment to about 10 students a year, but the new freedoms resulted in over 100 registered for classes in 1991. The seminary only had three or four professors, and each one also pastored multiple churches and mission points. The Union felt that T. should also pastor and encouraged him to begin an English-speaking international Baptist church in Bucharest. They began meeting in December 1991 and soon had a large attendance of expatriates and some English-speaking Romanians.

The Thomases filled the role of fraternal representatives during their two years in Romania. The Union was actively working on starting new groups and saw the IMB's role as supportive through training, financial support, and projects. T. worked closely with the Union and processed job requests for many future missionaries to enhance the work in Romania. They also began to focus their local ministry on the Roma community that was largely untouched by the gospel in Romania.[323] Due to growing differences with the IMB, the Thomases resigned in 1992 and joined the Cooperative Baptist Fellowship (CBF).[324]

Another veteran couple, Bill and Kathie Richardson, arrived in 1991 after many years of service in South America.[325] His specific assignment was theological education at the Bucharest Baptist Theological Seminary, which had been started with the assistance of the IMB back in 1923 when missionaries like the beloved Gills were around.[326] Richardson was well received by the Union leadership and assumed the role of fraternal representative when the Thomases resigned. The Richardsons, along with the Gerry Milligans who arrived in 1992, gave leadership to the International Baptist Church until the arrival of Mike and Kathy Kemper in 1994.[327]

Although none of the first families were primarily assigned to church planting, Richardson encouraged his students and the pastors to be evangelistic and to start new churches. He would often travel to new congregations to preach and encourage the work. He felt a special burden for a new church starting in Titu and personally invested funds to assist the congregation. He retold the story of a businessman who lost his briefcase with sensitive documents inside who feared for his job and possible consequences. The man shared his anxiety with a believing coworker who instructed him to "trust in the Lord and ask Him to lead." Soon the man received a phone call from a taxi driver who had found his briefcase. He shared his good news with his colleague and soon became a follower of the Lord and a member of the new church in Titu.[328] The Richardsons served in Bucharest until 1998 when they retired.

An interesting development in Romania during this period was the initiation of work among the Deaf. A Southern Baptist volunteer, Vesta Sauter, accompanied well-known Christian speaker Joni Erickson Tada to Bucharest in December 1989 to interpret her presentation for the Deaf.[329]

While in Bucharest, Sauter was invited to an annual meeting of Deaf clubs in Romania and connected with 24 presidents of clubs spread throughout the country. She returned the next year with a vision team of 16 workers, including several Deaf pastors, who divided into three teams and visited most of the Deaf clubs in the country. During the course of the next several months, five Deaf churches emerged.[330] Sauter and her husband, Mark, were later appointed by the IMB and assigned to the Czech Republic, where they influenced Deaf work throughout the region.[331] Now they serve as the IMB affinity leaders for Deaf peoples all over the world.

> An interesting development in Romania during this period was the initiation of work among the Deaf.

The work between the IMB and the Romanian Baptist Union returned to many of the historic priorities from the 1930s. The importance of developing the Union and the seminaries was key in the early 1990s, and the IMB fulfilled a major role in that process. IMB personnel also were key in connecting Union churches to eager partners in America with the result of hundreds of mission teams serving in Romania in the 1990s.

IMB workers in Romania continued to fulfill an along-side role with the national workers and helped influence the start of several churches in the latter 1990s. Jim Whitley worked closely with Moise Marin to establish Odel si Amenca Baptist Church in Bucharest, which was comprised of Roma.[332] This church has planted several other congregations in nearby cities and continues to be a strong church.

Since the Romanian Baptist Union had a vision for new churches, albeit very traditional ones, the invitation went to the IMB to send church developers or even "associational" missionaries.[333] Larry Carnes arrived in Romania in 1995 as one of these church developers. He said, "At that time, there was a spike in new churches as many mission points that had been established in villages were able to get legal recognition. It was not unusual for a pastor to have his primary church and five to 10 (or more) mission points/mission churches." Each of those mission points would have a deacon who filled in on the weeks the pastor was not there.[334]

In 1999, a new style of church was started. Against much criticism by the Union leadership, Vasile Talos started a cell church in Bucharest. He began with 30 members, which were divided into three groups. These groups met together for Bible study and ministry and then came together in a rented facility for Sunday worship. Within a decade, the church had grown to over 400 members and 30 small groups.[335] Carnes was in on this new style, too.

The IMB's most visible contribution to church planting in the latter 1990s involved a chapel building project. Don and Joyce McCauley led this project, which coordinated teams and funds from the United States. The mission teams traveled to Romania to conduct evangelistic events and finish the construction of a simple chapel facility. The local group of nationals had to secure the building permits, pour the foundation, and provide local volunteers to join the American volunteers.[336] The new churches related to mother churches, which often provided a pastor or elder to lead the new congregation. Unfortunately, the newly established churches did not often see the need to continue reaching into nearby towns to establish new work.[337] Fear of dependence prompted the IMB to discontinue the chapel building project.

For the past 10 years, the work in Romania has grown mostly among the Roma population.[338] Boyd and Jennie Hatchel led the local work among the Roma for many years and now give cluster-wide leadership for church planting among this group. Several new groups have been registered, and Roma workers are starting Roma Bible studies. A new Romanian church has been planted in Galati by Troy and Karla Geddes, and several new churches have been started in and near Craiova, under the influence of Bob and Diane Wagstaff. Personnel are again teaching at the seminary in Bucharest and are seeking to start a new church in the capital.[339]

# RUSSIA

George Lozuk grew up in a Russian-speaking home in Texas but served with his wife as IMB missionaries in South America for 30 years. But in 1991, they transferred to the land of his "roots" to establish fraternal relationships with the Union of Evangelical Christian–Baptists. The Lozuks moved to Moscow.[340] Though nearing retirement, the couple applied themselves energetically to the task of reopening relationships with Russian Baptists during their final term with the IMB. They were well received and respected by the Union leaders. In fact, Ballenger wrote, "The finest development, in my opinion, was our sending the Lozuks to Russia as our first personnel. They were experienced missionaries, dedicated, and called to serve in this unique situation."[341]

The Lozuks arrival was a celebrated day for the IMB. For the first time in IMB history, a residential missionary was able to live in Russia. Lozuk recalled the situation when he arrived in Moscow:

> *Baptist churches were already present (but very controlled)*
> *for some 100 years. Churches could only be started by*
> *permission of the Department of Religious Affairs of the KGB.*

> *The Moscow Baptist Church got permission to start five new churches in the city and used three deacons in each area to start the work. No company personnel were involved. My task was to relate to the Baptist work in Russia, Ukraine, Belarus, Estonia, Latvia, Uzbekistan, and Kazakhstan; meet their leaders; share the desire of Southern Baptists to cooperate and help in their ministries; and to get invitation letters from the national leadership to make possible the bringing in of new company personnel. The challenge to the nationals was to convince them that we could help and that we were true Bible-believing Christians. As new personnel were able to enter, they became gradually involved in the work of the church.*[342]

The basic strategy for starting churches in Moscow in 1991 was for assistant pastors or deacons from the one registered church (Central Baptist Church) to gather church members in the communities where they lived and start new churches.[343] In 1992, Billy Graham conducted a large evangelistic crusade in Moscow, and the Union arranged for 14 new groups to congregate following the event. About half of them survived to become new churches.[344]

The Billy Graham Crusade was just one example of pronounced changes occurring in the evangelical community of Russia. Also in 1992, the historic Union of Evangelical Christian–Baptist in the former Soviet Union dissolved, and a new voluntary Federation of Evangelical Christian Unions–Baptist was inaugurated.[345] Over a dozen new unions emerged immediately and counting satellite countries, eventually 25 unions would emerge in Eastern Europe. These changes accentuated the challenge in relating to newly established unions.

Norman and Martha Lytle transferred from Israel to a snowy Moscow in October 1992 to serve five years before retirement. Their first day was the same famous day that Billy Graham's evangelistic crusade started. Although they did not attend the first night, they did on Saturday and Sunday in the Olympic Stadium.

Fifty thousand people crammed into a stadium built for 40,000 on the final night. An additional 20,000 could not get in but stood outside in the sub-freezing temperatures to watch the event on a large screen. The final report declared a total attendance of 150,000 for the three-day meeting with 50,000 professions of faith.[346] The Lytles assumed the role of fraternal representative when the Lozuks returned to the United States for retirement. In this capacity, they traveled extensively, encouraging churches and their leaders.

Bob and Meg Tucker transferred from South America in 1993 and served a year in Moscow before transferring to Riga, Latvia, to lead the work in the Baltic states. Bob wrote, "All of my work was with churches already established and with the national Baptist conventions. I helped begin the seminary in Moscow and preached in many churches, but the churches were in such a survival mode that there was little thought in establishing new churches."[347] He focused on encouraging leaders and expanding their vision.

The first nontransfers to arrive in Russia were Mel and Nancy Skinner. Mel testified to a call to Russia a decade before the opening of the Soviet Union and his prayerful preparation for deployment.[348] They arrived in January 1992 and were the first to enter full-time language study in the country. While transfers arrived and largely served according to the Union's priorities of theological training and support roles, the Skinners prepared to work as church planters. It was difficult to begin work in this area because the pattern set with international workers was in other areas, and Russian leaders were not always encouraging of the establishment of new churches by non-Russians. Some of this related to control and mistrust, as well as possible doctrinal differences. Skinner reported, "Though it may sound critical, I would say that the churches in general are out of touch with Russian culture. They are not influencing society as a whole."[349] The new day in Russia brought a focus on re-establishing previous churches and solidifying the organization and its headquarters. Energy was placed in consolidation and clear structures for control.

Due to these many factors, church planting was not a priority for IMB personnel during the first half of the 1990s.

An example of the cooperation called for in the "Green Alert" was the organization of CoMission. It was an interesting multi-organizational initiative in Russia in the early 1990s. Spearheaded by Campus Crusade for Christ, the CoMission Project, or *JESUS* Film Project, was presented to the Russian Ministry of Education on November 5, 1992.[350] The film had been shown in several schools and was growing in popularity. The *JESUS* Film Project created a new department specifically to interact with the educational arm of the Russian government. It became known as the International School Project (ISP). About 80 Christian organizations joined the effort to show the film and introduce Christian ethics to the Russian school system.[351] A major challenge of the project was the description of the work as educational to Russians but as evangelistic to supporters in the United States. While cautiously optimistic at the outset, the Russian Orthodox Church became suspicious and eventually opposed the project. By February 1995, the Orthodox Church had convinced the Russian Ministry of Education to discontinue the project. Some believe that this possible duplicity contributed to the passing of more restrictive laws regarding foreign missionaries.[352] Though the IMB was not an initiator of the project, some IMB workers were connected with the showing of the *JESUS* film and follow-up in the Russian public schools.[353] The strategy concentrated on evangelism but was not instrumental in any widespread church planting in the country.

While the first several families appointed by the IMB to Russia settled in Moscow, by 1993 several missionaries arrived in the far-eastern city of Khabarovsk. Two teams formed with two different target groups. One team was comprised of three Korean-American couples—Chu Hon and Kei Yi, David and Elaine Lee, and Paul and Kathy Lee—and focused their energy on starting a Korean-Russian church.[354] They began holding services in a rented building with translation from Korean into Russian. Within a year, the group called Hope Baptist Church had about 25 in attendance.[355]

The young church continued meeting in the rented quarters for two more years. The David Lees and Paul Lees completed their two years of service toward the end of 1994 and returned to the United States. The Yis extended for an additional year and faithfully led the growing church. As a cardiologist, Yi worked at the Khabarovsk Medical Institute where he taught medicine.[356] He hosted over 20 doctors over the previous two years who had traveled to Khabarovsk to help with medical projects at the hospital.

Tragically on March 28, 1995, assailants entered the Yis' apartment and brutally murdered them.[357] Large sums of money were found in the apartment, so robbery was ruled out as a motive.[358] Such violence toward internationals was uncommon in the Far East of Russia, so speculation was common in the immediate weeks. The *East-West Church & Ministry Report* reported: "While police have not determined a motive, a South Korean source cited by *News Network International* speculated that the murders might have been committed by North Korean assassins."[359] The report also stated that the case would likely go unsolved because of a lack of evidence and the limited resources of the local police.[360]

The fledgling church was heartbroken by the murders but continued to faithfully meet and serve. The Yis had bequeathed a large sum of money to the little church, which enabled the congregation to purchase a building. The church still has a prominent mural of the Yis in their foyer and lovingly say that they were "built on the blood of the Yis."[361] Missionaries from Korea continued the work for the next decade until the church invited a deacon in the congregation to assume the position of pastor.[362]

While the Korean-American team worked among Korean speakers and some Russians, the second ministry team focused upon college students. As the group of five young adults met with the leadership of the Russian Baptist Union in the Far East, they were encouraged to reach the young people since the existing churches were largely ineffective in this area. The workers began teaching English in the university in the fall of 1993.[363] They also organized a student center, where they invited their new friends and acquaintances after class. The center opened in November with less than 10 in attendance. Two young Russian believers played the guitar and led the first programs in the center. The group planned a Christmas event, and 120 students attended. Though the gospel was presented, the students showed little interest.

A few months later, a winter camp was organized, and about 40 students attended. The gospel was clearly presented during two evening services, and, on the final evening, about half of the attendees responded to the gospel. The Russian Union leaders gave their blessing, the new believers were baptized, and a church was formed. One of the guitar-playing young leaders, Vladimir Lebedev, became the official church leader. Though often referred to by Russians as the "student center" or the "student church," the church was named Transformation Baptist Church and continued to be a vibrant church in Khabarovsk.[364]

Randy and Robin Covington arrived in 1995 as church developers and helped the young church to grow. They held worship services for several years at the Cooperative Technical School, which prompted many Russian Baptists to question the true church status of the group.[365] The Covingtons provided leadership training for Lebedev and also helped prepare Roman Alexeev and Igor Shubnikov as future leaders. Alexeev became the pastor when the Covingtons left for their first furlough and continued to serve in that capacity for many years.[366]

While the Covingtons were arriving in Khabarovsk, Paul and Lori Babb were moving to Almaty, Kazakhstan, to begin work among the 6 million Russians in that country.[367] About 10 years earlier, a new and vibrant church was formed in Almaty and named Comfort Baptist Church. This church had a vision for new churches and enlisted the Babbs' help in starting two new works. In 1995, a Bible study was started by Comfort Baptist Church in the Babbs' neighborhood, and they became encouragers for the deacon that led this new group. After two years, the group had grown large enough to constitute as Salvation Baptist Church. The mother church, Comfort Baptist Church, purchased a plot of land next door to the deacon's home and helped erect a modest building on the site.[368]

The Babbs were greater participants in a church launch in 1998 in Mayak, near Almaty. Under the missions umbrella of Comfort Baptist Church, they helped organize the showing of the *JESUS* film by hanging a sheet over the electrical wires that ran across one of the roads. A tent was soon erected as a point for distributing clothes to the needy and for conducting evangelistic services in the evening. Events and continued contacts grew over the next six months so that some seekers began driving into Almaty in order to visit the sponsoring church. Comfort Baptist Church again assumed the role of mother church and purchased a home in Mayak for a meeting place. Word spread that the home had belonged to a Muslim imam who had recently moved to Saudi Arabia. Soon a church was established in that home![369]

> Word spread that the home had belonged to a Muslim imam who had recently moved to Saudi Arabia. Soon a church was established in that home!

The IMB work in Novosibirsk, Russia, was opened by Charles and Phyllis Hardie. The Hardies served for nearly two decades in Taiwan before settling as IMB's first missionaries in Siberia in 1993.[370] Charles was well received by the pastors in Novosibirsk, and one of the leaders exclaimed, "They have finally sent real Baptist missionaries!"[371] Charles agreed with the stated priorities of the Russian Baptist leaders observing, "One of the great needs of Russia is teaching—teaching the pastors and teaching the leadership to reach their own people. There is a great need for evangelism, but who's going to do the changing of the spiritual diapers? It's easy to have babies, but who's going to take care of them?"[372] They applied themselves to language learning and started to share the gospel as broadly as they could. During their second year, Phyllis started a women's Bible study in their apartment. Several of the participants came to faith.[373]

The step of transitioning the Bible study to a church met strong resistance from the local Baptist leaders. Charles said, "The Russian Baptists were the greatest surprise. They were very strong about controlling the lives of their members. They had developed a system of control in order to detect any infiltrators into their fellowship. The pastors did not want the KGB to infiltrate the church and arrest the pastor in earlier days."[374]

The disagreement became so sharp that the leaders approached the mayor and asked him to deport the Hardies. Soon Charles traveled to Moscow in order to meet with national leaders of the Baptist Union along with regional IMB leaders. A move to another Russian city was discussed, but he felt that they would only serve one more term and did not want to start over again. He agreed to read a statement before the main congregation in Novosibirsk agreeing "to obey all 11 of the rules" passed down by the Union.[375] The Hardies' influence continued to grow, and a couple of new churches finally emerged along with some effective ministry among a growing segment of Russian society with an alcohol or drug addiction.

While the first major cities were opened by transferring missionaries in the early 1990s, a trend toward new career missionaries grew by 1993. Another trend was the sending of mature ISC missionaries (two- to three-year workers) to help begin new work. One ISC worker, Clay Cartwright, arrived in Tambov in 1995, about 300 miles south of Moscow. He worked closely with a new Bible study and encouraged the Russian leader. The next year, the group registered as a new Baptist church.[376]

While the first years in Moscow were dedicated to building strong relationships with Russian Baptist leaders and establishing the Union headquarters and new seminary, a significant shift began by the middle of the 1990s. The first appointees finished their full-time language study, and the first group of focused church planters arrived in the city.

In 1994, Mel and Nancy Skinner helped start a new Bible study group on the southern outskirts of Moscow.[377] The group grew steadily and registered as an official church in late 1995 with three Russian leaders.[378] Soon afterward, J. P. Manley began a youth Bible study in his home that quickly grew to over 70 Russian youth.[379] Though the Union was slow to recognize this vibrant body as a church, eventually it was constituted and accepted into the Union.

As in virtually every capital city in Eastern Europe, the first half of the 1990s witnessed the start of an international Baptist church by IMB personnel in Moscow. Brad and Lori Stamey arrived in the early 1990s as ISC workers and started an international English-language Baptist church.[380] They later returned and mentored Russian church planters, who started several churches in Moscow. Stamey was one of the few in Moscow to see a new church actually start another new church.[381]

Ed and Teri Tarleton and their four kids arrived in Moscow in the mid-90s and after language study, he began teaching in the Moscow Baptist Seminary. In the late 90s, he was asked to serve as mission administrator and stepped into the role of strategy associate by 2000. He has given leadership to the work in Russia since that time and has encouraged the acceleration of church planting and leadership development throughout Russia. He has been instrumental in keeping the vision consistent in Russia despite the turnover of personnel in this vast country.

Toward the end of the decade, Buck and Leslie Burch arrived in Russia and became influential church planters. After language study in Moscow, they moved to Bryansk. Burch had a gift for working with existing leaders and influencing them forward in church planting. He combined a visionary approach with the practical realities of the Union's posture and was able to see several new groups started in his city.[382] These were among the first reproducing churches that were directly started by IMB personnel.

During their second term, the Burches took their expertise from Bryansk to St. Petersburg and were soon asked to give strategic leadership for the IMB's work in that part of the country. The success in Bryansk was repeated in St. Petersburg with the birth of several new congregations.[383] Burch bluntly evaluated the early days of IMB church planting in Russia and gave three key reasons for the limited success: "the inexperience of personnel, the geographic uniqueness of Russia, and the limitation of personnel resources of IMB."[384]

The work in Russia continued to expand after 2000, and currently personnel are located in over 20 cities. New groups have been started in many of these cities with the greatest recent multiplication occurring in Ufa under the training of Chris Carr.[385] New people groups, like the Udmurts, were entered for the first time, and new Bible studies have been started among them.[386]

# BULGARIA

Bill and June Wardlaw transferred from Japan to Bulgaria in early 1991 to find a Baptist Union with about 15 small but strong churches started many years earlier by Russian Baptists.[387] Serving as fraternal representatives, the Wardlaws were well received by the Union leaders and asked to assist in many first steps following the new freedoms.

The first Baptist church in Bulgaria was established by Ivan Cargill of Russia in 1865, and the Union was organized in 1911.[388] The Union grew to about 3,000 members at the outbreak of World War II but steadily declined under communism. During the intervening decades, Christians were "killed, jailed, tortured, and persecuted mercilessly."[389]

The Union wanted to establish a training institute, reopen several churches that had been closed by the communist government, start new churches, and build new church buildings. Including church planting among their priorities was a unique plus in that part of the world in the early 1990s. Wardlaw wrote, "After 1991, new churches began all over the country. In particular, a couple of strong Gypsy churches began in the north. The challenges came from a combination of the Orthodox

Church and holdover communist opposition to new evangelical work."[390] Early personnel filled an auxiliary role in starting churches and were encouragers to the national churches that became mother churches.

As in several neighboring countries, many of the new churches were formed by the gathering of existing believers closer to their homes. Under communism, most church buildings in towns and villages were closed, and believers had to travel to the larger cities to attend worship. With the new freedoms, some abandoned church buildings were reopened, and many new congregations were started in homes of believers. Bruce Cassells noted, "The established churches did a good job of having new believers that had come to the cities go back out and start Bible studies and churches in their villages."[391] A priority for the Union was finding resources from abroad to build new sanctuaries for these small congregations. Cassells added, "Mistakes were made in feeling that they had to build large church buildings in these villages when simple small buildings or storefronts would have been better. Now many of these villages are depopulating, and these buildings are sitting almost empty."[392]

Though changes in the government were apparent at the start of the 1990s, many believers were still unsure if true freedoms would last and a true democracy would emerge. The Orthodox Church immediately reassumed favored status and often opposed new freedoms for evangelicals. Wardlaw called the reopening of the Baptist church in Russe a "great victory" in 1992.[393] It had been confiscated by the government years earlier and turned into a communist museum. The president of the Bulgaria Baptist Union, Theo Angelov, wrote of that momentous occasion:

> The confiscation of this church in the beginning of the 70s was one of many such actions of the communist authorities in our country. But the transformation of the church building into an atheistic club was an ultimate demonstration of power. It is not a problem for us to confiscate or just push a church building down. But to use God's temple as a club for atheistic agitation of the new faith—atheism—that was

*like slapping us with Stalin's hand, influencing the thinking
of a whole generation.*[394]

That same year, the Wardlaws encouraged the start of a new group in Sliven about 200 miles east of Sofia.[395] They traveled to the city several times to visit the apartment where the Bible study began, and this work was also encouraged by a journeyman, Spencer Stith.[396] After many years, the group grew and was established as a church.

Roger and Janice Capps transferred to Bulgaria from Asia in August 1993 and served in the area of theological education and pastoral training.[397] The period was characterized by an evangelistic zeal by the small Baptist Union and growing harassment by the government. Capps also described a period of great needs and humanitarian responses by the Union. This work included feeding the poor and the unemployed, as well as orphans. The Union also championed the defense of religious freedom and the protection of human rights.[398]

Later that year, the Orthodox Church gained influence with the government and used fear tactics to combat the "sects." The Wardlaws had to leave Sofia and searched for a city official friendly to their request for a visa. After being rebuffed twice, they settled in Stara Zagora and were able to secure a one-year visa. Several journeymen arrived and also had great difficulty securing a resident visa. Two were named in newspaper articles and labeled as "sect leaders."[399] The Wardlaws' visas expired in 1994, and they were denied renewals and were forced to depart the country by September of that year.[400] This refusal by the government prompted them to transfer to another assignment with the IMB.

Former journeyman Stith, along with his wife, Leslie, arrived in Bulgaria as career missionaries in 1998. He served as a strategy coordinator and developed a strategy plan for starting groups. He worked closely with the Baptist Union and saw some positive steps forward but unfortunately resigned early in their second term.[401] The work in Bulgaria saw a lot of turnover toward the end of the 1990s.

The work in Bulgaria continued to grow with the arrival of Bruce and Sophia

Cassels in 2002.[402] Bruce had served a previous term as a journeyman and met Sophia, daughter of a Bulgarian pastor. They later married and returned under appointment by the IMB. They have been well received by the Baptist Union and helped with the initiation of new work.

# 11

## POLAND

My wife, Susie, and I met Dagmara at a Christmas party in December 2007, just after returning to Krakow, Poland, for another term. Even after 16 years of missionary service, it never ceases to thrill us when God works in the life of a Pole. Dagmara was a neighbor of the Virklers, ISC workers. In her 40s, she was the mother of a young daughter. As a university English teacher, she immediately was interested in attending the English church service that would start in January 2008, but Dagmara also was intrigued by the gospel she heard at the Christmas party. With her 9-year-old daughter, they regularly attended the Sunday evening services and the Friday evening coffee houses. It wasn't long before Dagmara invited three of our journeymen to teach conversational English in her classes, which later led to an English Bible study discussion class. After having many conversations with her, Dagmara clearly stated her faith in Christ. I baptized Dagmara and two others at the same time in 2009, and she is living her faith and is active in a local Baptist church in Krakow.

Poland is a land that has suffered greatly in the past 100 years. Although Roman Catholicism continues to have a strong impact there, people are hungry for the gospel of Christ and discipleship. Cooperating from a distance and building relationship with the Polish Baptist Union in the 1980s, Jim and Becky Smith, who were IMB missionaries serving in West Berlin, often met with the Polish leaders during the late 1980s.[403] The first official request for personnel to Poland was in 1990 and resulted in the arrival of two journeymen and a reappointed couple by the end of the year.[404] The couple, Tom and Joyce Cleary, had served several terms in Austria before moving back to the States for a season. While serving in Austria, the Clearys made two mission trips to Poland and often prayed for the people of this land. They were reappointed by the IMB to teach English as an outreach in a new and growing English school in Wroclaw. Living in Krakow for a year in order to get a foundation in the Polish language, they became fraternal representatives during their first two years in the country and then asked that the title be given to other colleagues.

At the school where they taught in Wroclaw, the Clearys worked with other native English speakers. As the school was popular, prospective students would wait outside for up to three days prior to registration to ensure a place in the program. After a couple of years, a lottery system had to be established.[405] The school was housed in a newly constructed church complex, which also included a Bible seminary, book store, apartments for workers, dorm rooms for students, and guest room facilities. The location of the school in the Baptist church provided a clear identity with the local congregation, and several English students came to faith and were baptized into the membership of that church. The initiative to plant new churches in the city was not vibrant in the first half of the 1990s but would emerge in the second half of the decade.

Another important development of the work in Poland was the initiation of a partnership between the Polish Baptist Union and the Baptist State Convention of North Carolina.[406] A group of leaders from North Carolina traveled to Poland in 1989 and asked the Union about their dreams for the coming years. Union leaders shared their long-term vision of a Baptist theological seminary in the southeast suburb of Warsaw called Radosc. This land had been deeded to the Baptist Union by a converted Jewish man in the 1920s and had been the location of many "underground" youth and children's camps during the communist era.[407] Though the Union conducted seminary classes sporadically throughout the previous 25 years, it never had a dedicated facility or saw the opportunity for this dream to be realized. The North Carolina leaders accepted the challenge and started sending construction teams in 1990. The campus design called for a three-story seminary building, which included classrooms, library, office space, a dormitory for 30 students, a

> Susie and I were the first new appointees to Poland in the history of the IMB.

cafeteria, a large chapel, and a freestanding four-story apartment building that also included a conference center. The three-year partnership saw the completion or near completion of the apartment building and the conference center. The remaining projects were completed over the ensuing four years.[408] The seminary opened in 1994 with an inaugural class of 15 residential students.

The arrival of my family in April 1991 signaled the beginning of Polish-language work in the country. Susie and I were the first new appointees to Poland in the history of the IMB. Our appointment service in December 1990 at First Baptist Church in Charlottesville, Virginia, brought excitement and awe as we stood in front of the baptistery where the most famous IMB missionary, Lottie Moon, was baptized. We moved our three preschool children, Stephen, Celeste, and Meredith, to Krakow for two years of language study, but we also assisted the established Baptist church in the city by training Sunday school leaders.[409] (The Lord added Polish 9-year-old twins, Jacob and Eva, to our family in 2000.) I preached about once a month, and during the second year taught a monthly evangelism class for church leaders from south-central Poland. Susie helped start an outreach Bible study among young mothers, which met during the Children's Club conducted each Saturday at the church facility. We also started a home Bible study during our second year and saw four neighbors come to faith and be baptized.[410] The only Polish believing couple attending the home group developed a vision for evangelism and church planting and started the Second Baptist Church in Krakow about five years later.

In 1992, we were given the title of fraternal representatives, though we interpreted it differently than in most of the other Eastern European countries. We agreed to the liaison function of the role but continued to prioritize the role of church planting. In 1993, the pastor of Krakow Baptist Church, Gustaw Cieslar, was asked by the Polish Baptist Union to serve as president of the new seminary that was scheduled to open in Warsaw in 1994.[411] He agreed and asked me to accompany him to Warsaw to help start it up. I agreed only if church planting could stay my priority. We moved to Warsaw in June 1993. Soon I was asked to serve as academic dean of the seminary and worked alongside the seminary president in organizing a faculty and crafting a curriculum.[412]

The Polish Baptist Union had encouraged the move to Warsaw and the start of a second Baptist church in the capital city. Seeking the blessing of the first Baptist church's leaders in Warsaw, however, the process was more challenging than expected. They were not interested in the start of a second church. I had more than once heard that no city needed more than one Baptist church; no church could be started in a public, or unsacred, building; and NO FOREIGNER would EVER start a Baptist church in Poland.

I met two more times with the leadership council in order to further explain the need for additional churches and to assure the existing congregation that the new church would not "steal" members. During this time, I was contacted by a high school teacher who was interested in inviting a native English speaker to teach at his school. We met, and I proposed that Susie would teach two half days a week without a salary if the school would allow meetings to be held two times a week (Friday evening and Sunday morning) for free. The teacher and school officials agreed, and I met once more with the church council to share about the new opportunity. When the council heard the new developments and especially that the high school was across town from the existing church, and in a lower income part of town known as Prague, it gave its blessing.

Over the summer months, we cast the vision for new work in Warsaw among many different groups and individuals. Slowly a launch team of six Polish young adults came together. Among the group was a newly believing young couple whom I baptized during the first weeks of the church start. The other four were believers that were either new to Warsaw or had lived in the city for a couple of years without finding a strong church home. Ten thousand brochures were mailed in the neighborhood of the high school announcing the launch of the church and offering a coupon for a free New Testament. A volunteer team from the United States participated in evangelistic encounters in public parks, university dormitories, and in the hosting high school. These various events culminated with a group of over 30 gathering for the inaugural worship service in November 1993.[413] Attendance rarely slipped below that number, even though the group of volunteers returned to the States the next week. Soon, a Friday night youth club was added and was led by a journeyman, Scott Russell.[414]

News spread rapidly and visitors came. The worship style was different than in the evangelical churches of that day and very different from Catholic mass. It grew rapidly. This was the first Polish city with two churches, which set a pattern in the Union for the following few years. Within eight years, five cities would have multiple Baptist churches.

As the Polish Baptist Seminary opened in 1994, all of the students visited the new church and most attended it regularly during their three-year program. Not one of the students had ever seen a new Baptist church prior to their studies, which challenged them to see opportunities for new churches in their future service.

The time was ripe for such new expressions of worship and a more visible and aggressive approach to evangelism. Ivona Smolen had not been a believer long when she began translating for volunteers who served on projects in Warsaw. She quickly embraced this new vision for worship. "I started to build with them. I am full of enthusiasm. This church really meets expectations. It is open, ready to preach the gospel, available to those who want to serve God. The vision of the church is like it is written in the Bible. God will make a big thing in this church!"[415]

Soon after constituting as an officially registered church in November 1994, the church approached Wlodek Tasak, a youth pastor in the Gdansk Baptist Church, who began pastoring there in June 1995.[416] As we approached our first furlough, we reiterated often to the young church the five functions of the Church—worship, discipleship, fellowship, ministry, and evangelism—and that every healthy church should start another church within two to three years. We departed in June 1995, and Wlodek stepped into the role of pastor.

While on furlough in Houston, I called pastor Wlodek once a month to encourage and coach him as a young pastor. After about six months, he unexpectedly called me to let me know that eight members had prayed and felt led to start a new Baptist church in a part of Warsaw without an evangelical church. He quickly added that the group said, "It was Mark's idea." A third Baptist church was launched in the spring of 1996. When we returned to Warsaw in June of 1996, we worked with two other Polish leaders to launch a fourth Baptist church in the suburb where the new seminary had recently opened.

After about four years as pastor of Second Baptist Church, Wlodek resigned to become the editor of the Baptist monthly periodical, *Slowo Prawdy* (*Word of Truth*). The church called a young pastor, Sergiusz Borecki, who served for many years as pastor. Pastor Sergiusz rekindled the original vision of the church, and the church returned to the priority of church planting. As either initiating church or cooperating church, Second Baptist Church has been involved with the start of six subsequent congregations.[417]

Mark and Tatiana McNiel arrived in Poland in 1993, participating in the new church start while in language study in Warsaw. They deployed in 1995 to the northeast to help strengthen a mission station in Monki. Other workers soon followed the McNiels. In 1996, Doug and Marcy Shaw came to Poland and moved to Rzeszow, where they labored for several years to start a new congregation. Steven and Deborah Reece came in 1997 for language study in Warsaw and then moved to Gliwice in south-central Poland. After serving for a year in Kosovo following the war there, they returned to Poland to lead the team in Warsaw. They were instrumental in assisting a mission station in Otwock on the outskirts of Warsaw and helping it to develop into a strong, local congregation. Susan Carson arrived in late 1996 and was also a key member of the Warsaw team. Marc and Annie Byrd moved to Warsaw in 1998 and deployed to Czestochowa a year later. They saw a small, vibrant church officially registered by the end of their first term in 2002.

The work has expanded in Poland to several new cities. Most of the workers from the 1990s have either resigned or moved into other roles. The newly founded Second Baptist Church in Warsaw helped start six other churches in and around Warsaw over the next decade. Currently churches are being started in three Polish cities, and missionaries have arrived to begin work in two additional cities.[418]

# UKRAINE

As the rapid changes of the 1980s gained momentum, many observers saw the Ukrainian Baptist Union, which emerged as an independent union in 1992, as the strongest of all of the national conventions in the former Soviet Union.[419] Gregory Kommendant was serving as president of the Union of Evangelical Christian–Baptists in the Soviet Union until national unions were free to organize. He quickly returned home to Kiev, from Moscow, and gave leadership to the Ukrainian Baptist Union. He was an uncommon visionary at that time and quickly desired for the IMB to send personnel.[420]

Steve and Marilyn Haines were the first to arrive in 1991. They transferred from Colombia, South America, and he filled the assignments of professor of Church history in the new Kiev Baptist Seminary and fraternal representative to the Union. Haines found the Baptist Union had about 1,000 churches and perhaps 200,000 baptized believers (all adults). They were averaging the baptism of one new adult convert for every 12 church members when our SBC average was one for every 47 members, even counting our baptism of children."[421]

Ballenger reported on a meeting with Kommendant in 1991 and his honest assessment of the first wave of SBC volunteers. Kommendant affirmed the SBC and

IMB and shared his appreciation for the growing partnership and even valued the popular crusades that were being held. But he was concerned that preachers from America were exploiting them. "They come over, assemble a large group, which isn't hard to do; they preach one or two times and call people to respond with a promise of literature. Our people have been without literature for decades. Your preachers then go home and boast of their converts in the former USSR. This is exploitation. If you American Baptists cannot help us after the call to decision to gather these people and direct them to a training session and then stay long enough to help us initially instruct them, if you cannot do this, then we would rather that you not come."[422]

The IMB leaders listened and sought to connect early workers with the priorities of the inviting unions. Trying to balance the need for a rapid response to the new opportunities with the priority for prepared and qualified workers to appoint was a challenge in the early 1990s. Kommendant later reflected on the early partnership between the Ukrainian Baptist Union and the IMB: "Their influence was very important for the development of our Christian life in Ukraine. Working together with the largest evangelical denomination in the USA has been a great blessing."[423]

Though the relationships were good between Union leaders and IMB personnel, it wasn't always easy to work with churches due to the communist indoctrination that still remained. Churches were tightly controlled by the leader, rather than a congregational church government. Pastors were older and were not paid, since communists had always accused religious leaders of only wanting money. And three great differences in theology from the Southern Baptist model were pacifism, lack of security in salvation, and baptism necessary for salvation. The Union generally chose to focus on the commonalities with the IMB and welcomed the support and connection with partnering state conventions and churches. Ukraine had thousands of volunteers in the decade following the fall of communism.[424] Many of these groups conducted evangelism campaigns and provided construction teams.

Unlike many unions of that period, the Ukrainian Union had a strong plan for moving forward and had many partners, besides the IMB. Many Southern Baptist churches in the States worked directly with Ukrainian Baptists. Large crusades were organized and led by American evangelists throughout the country.[425] Though such events were not the priority of the IMB workers, they were often asked to help make introductions or connections so that such campaigns could be organized. It was also a physical impossibility for one or two IMB families to relate to the thousands of volunteers.

Haines added that the IMB was asked and agreed to help with the establishment of several seminaries, most notably in Kiev and Odessa, along with a home mission board.[426] The latter became the church-planting arm of the Union and was largely financed by donations from SBC churches. Though a comprehensive church-planting strategy was still being developed for the country, the Union genuinely wanted to see the establishment of many new churches.

Though church planting was not a primary assignment for the Haines, they were able to encourage the establishment of several new congregations. The first church start that they assisted was located in Kiev. A volunteer team from Texas was instrumental as it distributed thousands of fliers and tracts announcing the impending services in an old movie theater. Their efforts drew a crowd, and a church was formed and admitted into the Baptist Union within six months, which was the quickest acceptance of a church in the history of the Union.[427] Haines also wrote of new congregations started in Babintsi, Buda Babintsi, and Novi Zahlesnaya. Each had a unique story but shared the commonality of a deep spiritual hunger among Ukrainians and the commitment of some Ukrainian leaders.[428]

One local pastor Haines helped was Misha. The church Misha started pastoring hadn't baptized anyone for 40 years. Only 12 elderly people were left in the congregation. But God gave Misha a vision, and he immediately starting digging a foundation for a building that would seat 200 in a village of 800 people. Before long, they had their first baptism. Two hours before the baptism, spectators started arriving to watch, some in ox carts, some in tractors. Five hundred people witnessed that first baptism in 40 years. The excitement in the village overflowed to nearby villages, and several mayors gave land to the Baptist Union to start a church in their towns. Soon Misha was preaching five times on Sundays, leaving his home at 8 a.m. and returning after 10 p.m.[429]

Mike and Kay Norfleet had served in Asia and returned to the States for several years. They were reappointed to Ukraine in 1994.[430] They arrived as volunteer coordinators in Kiev to help give structure to the thousands of volunteers pouring into the country, and a year later Mike became mission administrator. "There was nothing attractive about the city or country. Yet we saw the vast need for hope and for the gospel. We also quickly saw the deep faith of the believers and their love for the Lord."[431]

> Five hundred people witnessed that first baptism in 40 years.

Some challenges in the work became apparent early in the 1990s. Due to the responsiveness of the Ukrainians, some took advantage of the situation for personal status. Also, while many volunteers were culturally sensitive and teachable, many others were intent on using an American-style approach to ministry. One interesting example was the unilateral decision by a prominent SBC church to plant a new church in Lvov, Ukraine. Without substantial dialogue with the Union or the IMB, the church invested great sums of money and pursued a path of church planting that was not culturally relevant. The venture was not successful and shut down not long after the start-up.[432]

Overall, however, the growth rate of the work in Ukraine was prolific in the middle to late 1990s. Missionary Mick Stockwell said, "The Union recorded an average of almost 10,000 baptisms and 150 new churches each year."[433] Due to the strength of the Union, the IMB's role developed as facilitators and trainers for much of the work. Stockwell added, "Approximately 100 new IMB personnel (both long and short term) came to join teams as a result of involvement on short-term mission trips. A high percentage of the approximately 1,500 new churches had some type of direct involvement of an IMB missionary or an SBC church in some way over the past 20 years."[434] This investment has been greatly valued by the Ukrainian Baptist Union.

Many other workers, like Keith and Jane Byrd, arrived in the mid-90s and served for many years alongside Ukrainian Baptists as catalysts and encouragers. Unable to serve in Belarus as first planned, the Byrds served faithfully in Dnipropetrovsk and later in Kiev.

The work in Ukraine continues to expand, and currently personnel serve in about 10 cities. Much of the emphasis is upon training national church planters, but several are still working diligently to start new groups in the major cities. The country is still one of the most open to the gospel, and the Ukrainian Baptist Union is still one of the strongest IMB partners in Eastern Europe.[435]

# 13

## BELARUS

Dan and Libby Panter served in Togo, West Africa, in the 1980s but always had a heart for the Soviet Union. After a visit, Dan kept praying for that part of the world. As the Berlin Wall fell and the region began to open, the Panters volunteered to transfer. Their offer was accepted, and they opened up the work in Belarus in October 1991.[436] The Panters were welcomed with open arms by Ivan Bukatyi and the other leaders of the Belarus Baptist Union. He was the fraternal representative and helped the Union enter the new day of freedoms.

Panter described a changing social setting which greeted their arrival: "The USSR was falling apart at the core, and the reverberations were felt worldwide. The economy was still the old Soviet system and everything was scarce but cheap. Monumental changes were brewing within the various Baptist unions, and a sense that freedom was coming was on every wind."[437] He encountered a Baptist Union that defaulted to its only known form of leadership, which was generally controlling and often untrusting. During the early 1990s, the government still closely monitored the activities of the Baptist Union.

The rampant poverty and physical needs were overwhelming. The nuclear disaster of Chernobyl in 1986 contributed to a spike of cancer, especially among children. The rate of thyroid cancer among children was 80 times the world average, and parts of Belarus had radiation levels that measured 40 to 50 times higher than normal.[438] The Panters had to secure ration cards to purchase basic necessities like bread, and a pair of shoes could cost a Belarusian a month's salary.[439] Many hours were spent daily in lines to simply survive.

The Union was not quick to trust international missionaries in the area of church planting but welcomed workers alongside as encouragers. Panter wrote positively of the Central Baptist Church in Minsk in the opportunity to encourage the leaders that launched a new church start. The subsequent IMB missionaries who arrived in the country continued in the same role as encouragers to the Belarusian leaders. The missionaries also, by default, served often as volunteer coordinators and processors of donations and gifts for the Union and churches.

The Panters were the only IMB workers in the country for the first two years, and rapid turnover would be a challenge in Belarus for the first decade. Panter named some crucial mistakes that were inadvertently made by early workers within and without the IMB, mostly concerning a lack of good strategy and pouring large sums of money into the pockets of leaders. The Panters' stay in Belarus concluded after two years when they accepted the role of strategy associate for Central and Eastern Europe and moved to Wiesbaden, Germany.

Several new workers arrived in Belarus after the departure of the Panters but likewise did not see the start of many new churches. Some missionaries encouraged national church starts and served as coaches or mentors to these church planters. Sporadic government interference hampered the work, and bureaucracy made securing a resident visa increasingly challenging. Unfortunately, most of the families that arrived in the middle of the 1990s did not serve a second term.[440] After the Panters left Belarus, others came for short periods of service until the arrival of Andy and Liz Leininger in 1997.[441] Leininger cited the start of five churches in the previous decade that had been influenced by IMB workers. He described these as traditional churches with a newly built chapel funded by the West that would hold 30 to 60 people.

A shift occurred in 2003. Reproducible church planting began with Dima L. and Good News Church. By 2009, six other churches were started in four cities. One of the second-generation churches has started a third-generation church. They are not 100 percent independently reproducible, but they are the best thing that has happened so far.[442] Leininger was influential in encouraging the Union toward this new model of church planting and helped combine a strong discipleship element into the process. They also stayed long term, from 1997 to 2005, which provided greater continuity to the work. They later transitioned to a leadership role in the Siberia region of Russia.

# CZECHOSLOVAKIA
## (Czech Republic and Slovakia)

The IMB related to Czechoslovakia with personnel in Vienna for many years and then with the Simmonses in Budapest beginning in 1989. Bob and Marsha Ford, after two terms of service in Scotland, transferred to Prague in 1991 to open the work in Czechoslovakia.[443] They assumed the role of fraternal representatives upon their arrival. They were welcomed by a secular culture excited about the new freedoms gained in its "Velvet Revolution" to throw off communism.[444] Dissident writer Vaclav Havel was elected as the first president and led the nation forward.[445]

The Baptist Union had about 3,500 members in 1993 when the country divided into two nations: the Czech Republic and Slovakia.[446] The Czech Republic kept about 2,300 of these members while approximately 1,200 lived in the territory of Slovakia. The Union did not have a strong vision for church planting or a great opinion of the IMB. Ford wrote, "At that time, the general secretary of the Czechoslovakia Baptist Union was very unhappy with the direction of the Board."[447] He spoke of a preference for workers in the newly formed CBF and considered restricting any further appointments of personnel by the IMB to the Czech Republic.

The only agreeable solution was for the Fords to plant an international English-language Baptist church. The Union leadership gave its grudging support, and the church launched around Easter 1993.

The church was founded as the International Baptist Church of Prague and met in the facilities of the main Baptist church in the city. Approximately 100 attended the first service, and the church experienced an exciting first year. The nature of international churches in Eastern Europe included a lot of transition due to work transfers and the mobility of expatriates. Ford said that the church had 25 to 30 core attendees with the remaining group being comprised of short-term contract workers and tourists. An interesting development in 1994 saw an influx of Chinese believers and seekers. Soon a separate Chinese-language worship service was started in another location.[448]

Although the English-speaking church had little impact among the nationals in Prague, there was influence in the lives of some university students who wanted exposure to English. After hearing the gospel, many came to faith. The Fords returned to the States for a furlough in 1995 and resigned to take a pastorate in Arkansas. The attitude of the Union was largely unchanged over the following decade, and the subsequent IMB workers had limited effectiveness in the country.

A breakthrough came when Mark and Vesta Sauter arrived in Prague in January 1997, expressly targeting the Deaf with the gospel.[449] Though hearing, Vesta's first language was American Sign Language. Mark also was fluent. They immediately began studying Czech Sign Language and connecting with the Deaf community in Prague and in surrounding cities. In 1999, they began storying through the Bible in the city of Brno, about 140 miles southeast of Prague. After 14 months, they had a small group of believers and several seekers who met regularly. This group became an official church in 2002.[450] They were given access to the Deaf school there and met regularly with a group for the next two years. About 12 responded to the gospel, and several others continued to attend the discussion group. The first believers were baptized in a bathtub, and this group became a church in 2004.[451]

The Deaf network was strong, and soon invitations came from other villages. The Sauters began to train nationals in sharing the gospel stories. Other IMB workers also began arriving in the latter 1990s to assist the Sauters with their work. Soon groups were recorded in Frydek-Mistek, Plzen, Hradec Kralove, Zlin, and eventually in Prague.[452] These groups were soon

> The first believers were baptized in a bathtub, and this group became a church in 2004.

transitioned to national leaders, and the Sauters moved to Budapest, Hungary, in late 2006. The work expanded in Hungary and several other nearby countries. The Sauters later moved to East Asia and were asked to give leadership to all of the Deaf work under the IMB umbrella.[453]

The first IMB appointees to Slovakia, Craig and Glenda Averill, arrived in 1995. They worked on strengthening relationships with the small, young Baptist Union. Their greatest impact was their investment in a young Slovak leader, Miro Misinec.[454] They mentored him and helped transition his small Bible study into a strong church. They also encouraged the work of two other mission stations and helped them grow into a mature church. At the Union level, the Averills were instrumental in a couple of publishing projects that produced *Experiencing God* by Henry Blackaby and two church-planting books by Charles Brock.[455] These projects were concluded before the Averills left the field in 2004.

A new group of church planters arrived after the turn of the 21st century, and the work moved forward slowly. After faithful sowing and repeated attempts at starting groups, the first Czech-language Bible studies began to emerge in the cities of Olomouc, Hradec Kralove, Brno, Prague, and Plzen.[456] New groups among the Roma also are being started in the Prague region of the country as well as Brno.[457]

The work in Slovakia has continued at a slow pace, though relations with the small Baptist Union continue to be positive. Tom and Sonya Holloway have served for a decade and have been well received by the national leaders. They are helping strengthen the few existing churches and continue to work on starting a new group.[458]

# 15

## LATVIA

Bob and Meg Tucker transferred from Canada to Moscow in 1993 and then to Riga, Latvia, in 1994.[459] Bob was asked to be the mission administrator for the North Europe Mission that stretched from Norway eastward through Finland and down through the Baltic states. He was the fraternal representative to Latvia, and also traveled frequently into Lithuania and Estonia. The small Unions in these countries did not have a clear vision for new churches, so the Tuckers concentrated on strengthening the work that was present.

He traveled to many churches and helped with some pastoral training during his three-year term in Riga. He said, "I preached in many of the churches, but the churches were in such survival mode that there was little thought in establishing new churches."[460] The Tuckers were joined in Latvia by Freddy and Deborah Davis in 1995 and Monte and Janet Erwin in 1996. The Davises transferred from Japan, and the Erwins transferred from the Caribbean.[461] Both couples felt that their role was to strengthen the existing work, and they were able to contribute through some training events, media projects, and the coordination of volunteer teams.

Though the IMB workers did not initiate church plants in the first half of the decade, they were able to encourage national church planters on a couple occasions. The Davises supported the efforts of the re-establishment of the Vilandes Baptist Church in Riga. Closed by the communist government in the 1940s, permission was received in 1995 for the church to reopen. The Davises helped with the music and some training for Sunday school workers. Upon completing their first term in Latvia, the Davises resigned from the IMB and remained in the United States.

The Erwins also contributed with some of the training in the Baptist seminary. Their background in curriculum development and teaching English was helpful, which was proving to be an essential component for theological education entering the 21st century. Responding to this Union need opened doors for greater cooperation and eventual church planting in their second term.

While seeking to serve according to the Latvian Union's requests and priorities, like teaching English at the seminary, the Erwins began to influence a new church start toward the end of their first term. In 1999, they met regularly with a young church planter and attended the first services of the Marupes Baptist Church. Though very small, the church was strengthened during the initial few months. The Erwins returned to the States for a furlough and during this period, the new church officially voted to join with a Reformed association of churches instead of the Latvian Baptist Union.[462] This was difficult news for the IMB, but church autonomy had to be respected. Within another four years, the church disbanded, and the members scattered to several churches. Many lessons were learned but unfortunately, no other churches were established by IMB personnel in Latvia. The Erwins resigned in the middle of the second term and returned to the States for ministry opportunities.

> Their background in curriculum development and teaching English ... was proving to be an essential component for theological education entering the 21st century.

The work among Latvians has seen slow progress over the past decade. Robert and Janice Mooney transferred from Africa and recently transitioned from full-time language study. The Union has a vision for many new churches, and the Mooneys are involved in helping start a new group. One recent, bright spot in the country is the work among Russian speakers in the eastern part of the country. Led by Gary and Cathy Ramey, several new groups have been started, and small, existing works have been strengthened.[463]

# ESTONIA

A spontaneous crowd gathered at the Tallinn Song Festival grounds for an all-night demonstration, which included nonstop singing.[464] This protest that took place on June 10 and 11, 1988, gave name to a movement in Estonia that is often referred to as the "Singing Revolution" (1987–1990). Soon parliament elections were held. This parliament passed an Estonian Sovereignty Declaration on November 16, 1988, and on February 23, 1989, the flag of the Estonian Soviet Socialist Republic was lowered to never again be raised. The blue, black, and white flag of Estonia was raised on February 24, 1989, and on May 8, 1990, the nation was officially renamed the Republic of Estonia.[465] The final Russian troops withdrew in August 1994.

A significant event for Baptists in 1989 was the re-establishment of the Estonian Baptist Union. The new Union began with 80 churches and 5,793 members.[466] The Union immediately began the laborious process of having seized properties returned from the government.

After several years of service in Brazil, Fred and Susan Ater answered the request to open the work in Estonia in 1993. The challenge of learning the language was even more difficult, because many people spoke Russian on the streets and in the stores in the early 1990s. The Aters were warmly welcomed by the small Estonian Baptist Union. The Aters served as fraternal representatives and helped in several areas requested by the Union leaders. They provided training for pastors and Sunday school leaders and were instrumental in a publishing project that utilized thousands of dollars from the IMB to publish and print new Christian books in Estonian. The Aters also helped lead a strong partnership between the Union and the Baptist General Convention of Texas (BGCT). This multi-year partnership included many volunteer teams, summer missionaries, and construction projects throughout Estonia. The Alters resigned from the IMB in 1999 to take a ministry role in the States.

In 1994, the Allika Baptist Church in Tallinn was reopened and the next year saw the planting of a new church in Tallinn called Mustamae Kristlik Vabakogudus.[467] Church planting was not a high priority for the newly established Union, which was still trying to grow in strength and solidify its organizational structure.

Though the Baptist Union of Estonia was open to a new family to follow the departure of the Aters, five years passed before the next family arrived. As mission administrator who supervised the countries around the Baltic Sea, I visited the Union each year and helped connect the leaders to volunteer teams in the United States. I also kept the job request in Estonia as a high priority in the IMB's work in that part of the region.

It would be nearly five years before the arrival of Tom and Jennifer Thompson in 2003. The Union welcomed them warmly and had few expressed expectations for their ministry. They worked hard to learn Estonian and have slowly earned the trust and respect of the leaders. Overtures by the couple toward church planting were not fully embraced until a discussion emerged about a possible international church in Tallinn. The Union encouraged this step, and an English-speaking international Baptist church was established in the capital city in 2008. A second one was recently started in the second largest city in the country, Tartu. Unfortunately no Estonian-speaking church has been directly planted by IMB personnel.[468]

# MOLDOVA

It was a long-awaited day when the small country of Moldova emerged from the Soviet Union in 1991 with a small Baptist Union ready to aggressively evangelize and plant new churches.[469] In consultation with the Union leadership in 1995, it was decided that the country of 4.5 million would be divided into three partitions, and an IMB church planter would be placed in each region. Joe Saunders and Ken and Mattie McLemore arrived that same year. Saunders served a three-year term in the central region. The McLemores moved into the southern part of the country and concentrated their work alongside national workers. In 1996, Tom and Tammy Fox and Richard and Carmela Bartels deployed to the northern city of Balti.

Baptist leaders were glad to welcome partners, but their history of communism prompted an uneasy trust at the beginning. This mindset represented the society at large. Though many were curious and interested in welcoming Americans, others were skeptical and uncertain. Despite this inherent distrust, the McLemores found the Moldovans open to the gospel when they were able to share at a spiritual level. In their part of the country, they felt unable to initiate new groups or churches but encouraged the work of the Baptist Union. They were told that the Union had recently had some negative experiences with Western missionaries so were cautious to remain in a support role. Ken was injured in a household accident, and they resigned to return to the States at the end of their term in 1998.[470]

The Bartels transferred from Benin, West Africa, where they had served for 16 years.[471] They were one of the few IMB workers in the country who studied the Romanian language, sometimes also called Moldovan. The Bartels encouraged national church planters during their two terms of service but felt most comfortable in the area of teaching and training. They led some pastor/leader training seminars and also taught a couple of courses in the training institute in Chisinau. Because of communism, Christian brothers and sisters had either remained faithful, even at the cost of imprisonment, or had denounced their faith. The basic challenge centered upon faithful Christians forgiving the others or working toward restoration.[472] This dilemma improved over time but was a difficult barrier in the early 1990s. The IMB workers tried to help bridge this gap and work with all willing partners.

While church growth was seen throughout Moldova, the greatest growth of new congregations in the latter 1990s was seen in the northern region of the country. In the early 1990s, the area had a population of 1.2 million with four Baptist churches. A couple of these churches were strong, and the historic church in Balti had well over 1,000 members. By the end of the decade, 27 new churches were planted, and IMB workers were directly involved with five of these.[473] Fox shared of a key young couple who teamed with him in starting the new congregations. The husband, Sasha, was from a believing family but was not actively sharing his faith. His young wife, Svetlana, was not a believer when they met in college in Chisinau. Soon after they married, she came to faith, and they moved back to her hometown of Cupcini in northern Moldova. Her father was so enraged by her conversion that he tried to kill her![474] The Lord began to work greatly in their hearts, and they started inviting friends over for Bible study. Soon four of their friends embraced the Lord.

Fox met this young couple in the winter of 1996 and began investing in them and casting a vision for the northern region of Moldova. They planned an evangelistic campaign in their town; five people responded to the gospel and several others joined the Bible study. While establishing this new group in their faith, Fox encouraged them to take the gospel to the nearby town of Edinet. The believers at a vibrant church in Balti sent their youth group to help promote an evangelistic event. The combined groups personally contacted over 15,000 people in this town of about 25,000.[475] The leaders met with the mayor and secured permission to hold the outdoor meeting in front of the culture club. A final trip was made to the electric company and for a fee of about $2.00, the workers agreed to leave the electricity on for the sound system.[476] A "good crowd" heard the gospel. One repented and several others signed up for the new Bible study group that was forming. The Bible study began meeting the next week, and soon a group of three to four from Edinet was meeting and being led by believers from Cupcini.

> Ironically, they were finally able to secure a room in the Communist Party hall.

While the leaders were discipling several seekers to conversion, Fox continued to cast a vision for the next town that needed a Bible study. The groups from Cupcini and Edinet traveled 22 miles north of Edinet to Briceni, located near the Ukrainian border. Soon they discovered a young believer who had been a classmate of Sasha's in Chisinau. She helped open some doors and brought credibility to the new group. The general reception in the new location was cold, and the group was greatly restricted and required to meet indoors. The group rented a room in a public culture house, but it was unheated; they had to move after winter arrived. They then rented a room in a music school, but pressure was applied to the director to force them to move out. Ironically, they were finally able to secure a room in the Communist Party hall.[477]

Due to the distance and greater resistance in Briceni, the group expanded slowly and took several years before it was officially recognized. City officials forbade street evangelism and public events, though the group continued canvassing neighborhoods and parks. After years of saturating the town with the gospel, breakthroughs finally came around the year 2000. Several years of multiple baptisms followed.

While traveling out to Briceni once a week, the believers from Cupcini also started new outreach Bible studies in their town. They continued to pray for outlying towns that did not have an evangelical church. In 1999, Fox cast a vision for the town of Soroca, located near the Ukrainian border. Regarding this city, Fox wrote, "Soroca is a unique city in the world. It has a population of about 40,000 people. The king of the Romani (Gypsy) people lives there. It was also the home of a fortress established by King Stefan the Great."[478] The group planned their first evangelistic event, including street preaching, in the fall of 1999. Within a year, the first baptism was scheduled with 23 submitting to believer's baptism in the Dnestr River. Nearly 700 attended the public baptism.[479]

The final location targeted in the late 1990s was the town of Lipcani. Located near the Ukrainian and Romanian borders, the town was known for its 600-inmate children's prison. Fox spoke to a small home group there in 1997 but perceived that the group was not trying to reach neighbors in the city. He tried to balance the role of the existing believers with a model of church that is more evangelistic and less controlling. After several years, a church was established in the town.

Fox calls this a "time of harvest" in Moldova. His strategy? Gospel saturation in the form of street evangelism, neighborhood canvassing, public meetings, and the establishment of Bible studies. He also utilized groups of volunteers from the States for large outdoor events, which would attract many from the towns. Fox underscored that the thrust of every volunteer group was evangelism and grouping.

Another key that he discovered early was the impact of public baptisms. For convenience, he scheduled the baptism of the first convert in Briceni in another town but realized his mistake. He vowed to always baptize the new converts publically and locally because of the witness. Lastly, he saw some of the greatest growth in these new groups while he was in the States on furlough. He concluded that investing in the leaders early prompted the ongoing cycle of growth and new groups.[480]

The missionaries in Moldova largely worked themselves out of a job. The small country has a vibrant, evangelistic Baptist Union, which has a vision for church planting in their country and internationally. The IMB presently has one family, Chris and Nancy Russell, in Moldova seeking to encourage the Union's strong vision and help train both domestic and international church planters.[481]

# 18

## LITHUANIA

Not exactly sure what they were getting into, Milton and Lara Magalhaes arrived in the newly formed Lithuania in 1995, infant daughter in arms. They knew it wouldn't be an easy place to live because just a few months before, the first IMB missionary couple to enter that country left after only staying a few months. With determination and courage, the Magalhaeses came to the southernmost Baltic state with a population of about 3.5 million. It declared its independence from the Soviet Union on March 11, 1990, which prompted a Soviet economic blockade. The hostilities escalated, and the Soviet military attacked the Vilnius television tower in order to control the airwaves. Lithuanians resisted the takeover, and 13 were killed by the soldiers on January 13, 1991.[482] Soon international recognition came for the independent country, and the last Soviet troops withdrew on August 31, 1993.[483] Throughout the chaos, economic hardship of the country, the blessing of a second baby, language study, and a lack of a cooperative spirit from the Baptist Union, all in their first term, the Magalhaeses survived and are still faithful IMB workers there.

They first settled in the coastal town of Klaipeda to study the language. The small Baptist Union had five churches and was extremely controlling of partners.

After several years of struggling and attempting to work together, the IMB decided to bless the Union and to start new churches, even without their cooperation.

In 1998, the Magalhaeses moved to Silute, 40 miles southeast of Klaipeda. After sharing the gospel, several came to faith in the initial months. Two lay leaders emerged in the town, one a soccer coach and one a policeman. The first Bible study was held in the IMB couple's home in December 1998. Through active evangelism, the group steadily grew and was able to register as an official church in the spring of 2000.[484] As the Magalhaeses went on their first furlough, Rimas Celiauskas, the soccer coach, became the bivocational pastor of the church. This church grew rapidly in the early years and became a catalyst for helping start future churches in Klaipeda and even in the capital of Vilnius.

During their second term in Lithuania, the couple supported a new center in Klaipeda for the rehabilitation for those with alcohol and drug addictions. Several residents responded to the gospel, which prompted the start of another new church. The Silute church worked closely with them to initiate this new work in 2001. A former resident in the program, Emanuelis Kinas, embraced the gospel and was mentored by Magalhaes. He grew in the faith and became the pastor of the new church that was officially registered in 2007.[485]

The Silute church continued to grow in the early 2000s and conducted evangelistic events in several outlying towns and villages. Some people responded to the gospel, and a few groups were started. Though the groups did not transition into churches, several of the converts later became active members in other evangelical churches. The Silute church and the young church in Klaipeda, called New Hope Baptist Church, often worked together to conduct evangelistic events and camps. They have also been a great help to the Magalhaeses, who moved to Vilnius to initiate another church start in 2006.

The new church in Vilnius is called Capital City Evangelical Baptist Church. The work moved slowly in the beginning years with a small group of newly baptized believers and a group of seekers who gathered on Sundays for worship. While concentrating much of their energy in Vilnius, the Magalhaeses continued to engage other new towns and cities with the gospel. New small groups were formed in Kaunas, Saugos, and Klaipeda.[486] Magalhaes described these young churches as "very evangelistic, mission-minded, supportive of one another, and striving to reach their communities for Christ."[487]

Investing heavily in developing national leaders in their new churches, this persevering couple continually cast a vision to evangelize locally and in surrounding towns. They also have utilized many volunteer groups from the States who have come and conducted evangelistic events like crusades, camps, and concerts. In 2008, they began a strategy called "12 by 12," which emphasizes the start of 12 new churches in the next 12 years.[488] In this traditionally Roman Catholic culture, which is often cautious about new ideas, the Magalhaeses have modeled persistent evangelism and longevity to plant churches and initiate a growing network of evangelistic Baptist churches.

> ... they began a strategy called "12 by 12," which emphasizes the start of 12 new churches in the next 12 years.

ALBANIA

"To say that Albania is unbelievable is an understatement," wrote Mary Carpenter in a letter to IMB missionaries appointed with them in the Clemson University coliseum in April 1992. "I am looking out the window at my wash. I started a load at 9 a.m. and finally gave up and took it out at 2 p.m. The small apartment where we live is … up four floors. The first night, I really wondered if I could do this, but each day has gotten a little better," she wrote, three days after their arrival in the country.[489]

Albania was one of the last Eastern European countries to open its borders and allow IMB residential workers. The first record of believers' baptism in Albania dates back to 1937, though details are scarce regarding the early missionary endeavors. The IMB engaged in daily Albanian radio broadcasts throughout the 1980s.[490] Known as the "most atheistic country in the world," no Baptist union or registered churches existed when a "window" was finally open after strict communist control. The EBF immediately began to coordinate the entrance of Baptist groups into the country in 1992.[491] Soon the Albanian Encouragement Project began with 25 founding mission agencies, including Campus Crusade for Christ, Youth With a Mission, Operation Mobilization, and Trans World Radio, all working together to coordinate efforts to reach the country with the gospel.[492]

The country was possibly the poorest in Europe in the early 1990s, and many of the first responses and projects were related to humanitarian aid. On April 8, 1992, a shipment of 270 tons of flour was sent by the coordinated efforts of the SBC, Canadian Baptists, and the Baptist World Alliance.[493] Survival was the priority for Albanians emerging from a dictatorship.

While raising their young family in Texas, David and Mary Carpenter became aware of the plight of Albania when J. T., their elementary-age son, solicited his mom and dad to pray with him for a people group who lived in Albania. David, a lawyer, and Mary, a professor, began to also acquire the same heart for Albania as their young son. Eventually, they dropped their lucrative careers and, following God's call, were appointed as the first IMB missionaries to Albania, serving in the Cooperative Services International (CSI) branch. They and their three children moved to Tirana in September 1992, where they worked with other Great Commission groups to help bring the gospel to this once completely closed society.[494]

With conditions being so difficult, survival initially took up much of their time. Water was only turned on by the city for one hour at 4 a.m. each day. That meant they had to collect the trickle of water in the middle of the night in whatever containers they could find. The water collected would have to be boiled for drinking, bathing, and washing clothes and dishes. And there would be days the water never came on. Electricity was sporadic. Food was difficult to find. The best food they found early on was from surplus food shipped by the United States troops after Desert Storm. It beat buying the cow's head Mary reported seeing in the sparsely stocked market their first week![495]

In their first term, David's law experience allowed him to participate in having some influence in the new constitution that was being written for Albania's new government.[496] A year after the Carpenters arrival, Gerry and Arylis Milligan transferred from the Middle East to Romania in 1993 and agreed to help with the early work in Albania in 1994.[497] Other workers in that initial wave included Bill and Debbie McIntyre, Gale and Leslie Hartley, and Charles and Bonnie Wiggs.

The Milligans were both trained nurses and were specifically asked to help set up a nursing school in Albania.[498] They arrived in September 1994 to a country still "out of order." Many official buildings, like schools, were abandoned, and every valuable piece of furniture or intact fixture had been removed or vandalized. They recalled that "anarchy" seemed to reign throughout Tirana.[499] Only two evangelical churches were open in the capital city, led by expatriates. One was pastored by an American from an Assemblies of God background, and the other was led by an American from an Independent Baptist background. Both churches had services in English with translation into Albanian.[500]

By the end of 1994, Gale and Leslie Hartley were appointed by the IMB and arrived in Albania as new missionaries.[501] They also were shocked by the third-world nature of the country upon their arrival. Hartley recalled, "Garbage was literally everywhere. The roads were totally in disrepair, and the city infrastructure was almost nonexistent. Food was scarce, crime rampant."[502] To contrast the physical condition, Hartley remembered an amazing openness to spiritual conversations. He

> "I've heard about the Bible, but I've never seen one."

often would be engaged in conversation with strangers in the market who would immediately show interest in studying the Bible. He remembered an exchange with a Muslim man on the street to whom he offered a Bible. The man responded, "I've heard about the Bible, but I've never seen one."[503] He received it gratefully, and Hartley was able to share the gospel fully with this seeker.

After some intensive language study, Hartley began traveling out from Tirana seeking places to begin Bible studies. He connected with six cities where people enthusiastically responded to his invitation and asked him to lead a group. He began by traveling to the cities of Fier and Girokaster frequently to lead new groups.[504] He saw about 20 conversions in these two towns and had the joy of baptizing these new believers.

A major project was also initiated in the summer of 1994. The Carpenters' team joined with Campus Crusade for Christ and a Swiss mission agency, Helimission, to plan Project AERO (Albanian Evangelical Rural Outreach). About 50 partner churches and agencies joined in this massive effort to present the *JESUS* film and distribute Bibles into every village in Albania.[505] Over 15,000 people in 175 villages came to watch the movie. More than 2,300 professed faith in Christ as a result. College-age volunteers from Baptist Student Unions in the United States assisted, while Helimission provided helicopter transportation to and from the camps where the students lived.[506]

Follow-up was provided by 22 ISC workers over a three-year period with the hopes of starting new Bible studies and churches.[507] Charles and Bonnie Wiggs had retired from the IMB after 32 years of service in Korea but agreed to help give administrative support to this project in the villages. They wrote about the events of that summer and the following months: "Following the summer emphasis of showing the *JESUS* film in hundreds of villages, our team revisited those villages and did discipleship training for the rest of the year."[508] Many Albanians responded to the gospel, and some ongoing groups resulted from the campaign. Also, the Lord used Project AERO to prepare future Albanian missionaries, who are presently serving not only in Albania but also in Turkey and Macedonia.[509] Carpenter wrote during that time, "Our goal has always been to see multiplying disciples who will begin churches. After months of discipleship, we have seen many baptized in recent days. We believe that the gospel will spread throughout the country by the efforts of these and other new believers. That is a real blessing to us!"[510]

During their last month on the field before furlough, the work of the Carpenters officially transitioned from CSI leadership to the mainstream IMB in July 1996.[511] The Carpenters did not return to the field after their time in the States and resigned from the IMB to fulfill a role in a new ministry.

In early 1997, civil unrest grew in Albania due to an economic meltdown. Many ambassadors were recalled, and United Nations troops were deployed to restore order. The Hartleys evacuated to Bosnia for a year and later to Croatia for a year. They returned to the United States in 1998 and resigned from the IMB.[512]

Among the small group of missionaries returning to the country after the evacuation was Lee Bradley. He worked hard to learn Albanian and labored faithfully to plant a new church in the Tirana suburb of Laprake.[513] He later helped coach other successful church starts in Tirana. A fellow worker, Suzanne Lacy, assisted a church plant in the city of Elbasan that continues to meet. After many years of service in the country, Bradley had an insightful perspective on Albania that church planting was and is a harder task than evangelism.

According to Bradley, people in Albania are polite and respectful of foreigners. They will listen to a gospel presentation and even attend a Bible study or meeting. However, getting them to make a solid commitment for the long term is harder. Some have asked what works in church planting. Many

*" ... the key for anyone serious about church planting is to be serious themselves and make a long-time commitment to one community and live there."*

different strategies have been tried by a variety of missionaries: English, computers, open-air evangelism, door-to-door witnessing, small group Bible studies, rental of a place with an announcement to come and worship, medical clinics, community-development projects, agricultural projects, humanitarian aid, publishing, and radio. Each of these strategies has had some degree of success in helping gather and filter people. Most missionaries will say that these strategies are mostly a means to an end. Bradley reinforced that "the key for anyone serious about church planting is to be serious themselves and make a long-time commitment to one community and live there." Being a daily presence in a community is the way that Albanians take the gospel seriously. The places where missionaries have invested seven to 10 years are the places where the churches have taken root and grown. Although there are

145

a few exceptions, those places where missionaries have come once a week or where they come from other cities to work in the village for the day do not have long-term success. He stressed that relationships and faithfulness are the keys.[514]

Albanian Christians have not developed the natural vision for planting new churches, and this unfortunate side effect has hampered the continued growth of the church in the 1990s. Bradley has tackled this problem head on. He has continued faithfully in Albania to the present. The bulk of his work over the last decade has concentrated on the establishment of a training center for Albanians. He leads this center, which equips Albanians to start and lead groups. The work in the country has steadily grown over the past decade.[515]

# 20

## LESSONS LEARNED FROM THE WALL

**E**xperience is everything. You don't know how things are going to work out until you've been through it. I'm so grateful the Lord is with us every step of the way.

The amazing investment of IMB personnel in the former Soviet Union provides informative observations concerning failures and effective, fruitful ministries. Prior to 1988, the IMB had only 10 missionaries assigned to the Eastern Europe mission and only one living behind the Iron Curtain.[516] By 1990, 12 missionaries were under appointment with five securing residential visas in the former Soviet Union sphere. By August 1991, 49 were under appointment, and over half had already arrived to live in Eastern Europe.[517] This deployment grew over the following decade and literally changed the face of the work in Eastern Europe.

As history was unfolding in Eastern Europe during the early part of the 20th century and the latter part, Southern Baptists in different generations sensed a new day dawning but were not sure how best to respond. The pleas by IMB leaders just after World War I and just after the Berlin Wall fell were the same—send personnel to Eastern Europe to bring good news. In April 1990, the IMB's president, Keith Parks, voiced a passionate request to the trustees just three months after the cruel Ceausescus of Romania had been executed Christmas Day. "God has given to Southern Baptists much wealth," said Parks. "We will be more guilty than the Ceausescus [if] we shamelessly wallow in self-indulgent luxury while a lost and dying world goes into eternity with no knowledge of Jesus Christ. This is God's right time. Will historians look back to say the last decade of the 20th century Southern Baptists could have led the way—but at God's right time, they did wrong?"[518]

The initial 12 years of service in the territory of the former Soviet Union brought diverse observations to the scores of missionaries who initiated or early joined the work of the IMB in these countries. These observations are generally neutral in character but are still instructive for current missiologists.

## Value of celebrating historic breakthroughs

Believers throughout Eastern Europe, whether in the frozen tundra of Siberia or the more temperate climates of South Europe, taught newly arrived IMB workers the value of celebrating the new freedoms of the era. Part of their joy was shown by welcoming missionaries from America who could help them to actively re-establish their churches. The return of confiscated church buildings also heightened the joy of the national believers. Theo Angelov, leader of the Bulgaria Baptist Union, wrote in the late 1990s that Baptist Union leaders had repeatedly asked government officials in Russe if they would return the seized Baptist church building. "This building will never be given back for religious use," the official stated. "But in 1991," said Angelov, "we got the building back. We opened the ... door, and the whole building was empty ... The baptistery was cemented." Circling up, the 15 believers offered a prayer of thanksgiving to God. "At that moment, I ... sensed a hand far above us writing a new page in the history of the Baptist church in Russe, a new page in the history of the evangelical churches of Bulgaria, and probably one of the final pages in the history of communism in my country. It was like a dead body ... resurrected for new life again."[519]

The return of properties and the greater freedom to worship publically and unhindered were clear signs of the new day. Early reports emerging from the crumbling Soviet Union celebrated massive crowds at special events. Reports from the area in 1990 told of evangelistic rallies "all over the USSR. In Bulgaria, 1,000 attended and 10 made decisions; in Czechoslovakia, 10,000 attended and 1,000 made decisions; in Estonia, 20,000 attended and uncounted hundreds made decisions. In Romania, a church of 2,500 baptized 400 last year, and the first three months of liberty started 20 chapels."[520] The early 1990s were unprecedented days of joy in the churches of Eastern Europe.

## Reality of a changing IMB entering a changing Eastern Europe

The changes of Eastern Europe toward the end of the century were front-page news. Yet, equally important in the equation that brought the IMB together with the unions of Eastern Europe were the changes taking place at the IMB. While many Baptist unions and churches in the former Soviet Union stepped into the new day with open arms for American Christians, others were not sure about the commitment level of their distant brothers and sisters. George

> This skepticism sometimes prompted a trial period prior to acceptance of personnel.

Lozuk reported that part of his responsibility in Moscow was "to convince leaders that we could help and that we were true Bible-believing Christians."[521] This skepticism sometimes prompted a trial period prior to acceptance of personnel.

Another byproduct of the opened borders was the possibility to travel and emigrate. Many national Baptists and pastors quickly emigrated to the West when given the opportunity. Tom Fox shared that this was especially challenging in Moldova. In one church alone, several large families immigrated together to the United States, and the church lost about 40 percent of its membership in one year.[522]

The IMB was undergoing momentous changes at the end of the 20th century as well. As the first personnel arrived to live in Eastern Europe in 1988, the IMB was applying the "70/30 Plan" to missionaries, in which the majority of their time would be spent in church planting.[523] The previous priorities of the IMB in earlier days of cooperation in Romania, Hungary, and Yugoslavia had been theological training, general education, and development of a Baptist union. Some unions had these same expectations as the door opened once more to cooperative work.

The already documented controversy over the IMB's defunding of the International Baptist Theological Seminary in Ruschlikon, Switzerland, affected the relationship of missionaries with the unions of Eastern Europe in the 1990s. The EBF and almost every Baptist union in Western Europe broke relations with the IMB.[524] Though less in some Eastern European unions, the animosity was still very real toward the IMB trustee decision.

An example of a strong reaction against the IMB's decisions of the early 1990s was the Czechoslovakian Baptist Union. Soon after the arrival of the Fords, the Union's general secretary bluntly stated that he would not support the planting of any churches through the ministry of Southern Baptist missionaries.[525] Such relationships inhibited strong partnerships and progress toward the establishment of new churches.

For some unions, this disillusionment grew with the announcement of the "New Directions" restructuring of the IMB in 1997 under the direction of Jerry Rankin.[526] Though motivated by a Great Commission vision to make disciples in every people group and accelerate the rate of evangelism and church planting throughout the world, Baptist leaders understood a decreased amount of consultation with the IMB and a lesser investment in existing work. Many of them also saw a move toward independent work since the IMB "had not consulted with them sooner."[527] In Romania, Preston Pearce recalled, "We found the Baptist Union struggling to adjust to the IMB's return to sending rather than funding missions. They were facing severe economic challenges and were puzzled by our resistance to funding various good projects."[528] The paradigm was shifting away from the support of ongoing work with the push toward frontiers and unengaged people groups.

## Rise of immigrant churches

The Soviet Union and satellite countries prided themselves on their tight border controls, which limited the entrance of foreigners and the exit of nationals. By the late 1980s, the borders were rapidly opening, and the largely unexplored West beckoned many from Eastern Europe. The immigrant population of Europe grew to over 70 million in the 20 years that followed the collapse of communism.[529] Though some of these immigrants were from outside of Europe, a large percentage migrated from Eastern Europe to Central and Western Europe. Some immigrants began new churches, and many were evangelized and grouped into new congregations. The largest church in Europe, located in Kiev, was founded by a Nigerian, as was the largest congregation in London.[530]

Many missionary agencies began targeting these growing populations with the gospel and started ethnic churches among the various groups. In his article, "The Mission of Migrant Churches in Europe," Jan Jongeneel wrote of a clear distinction between the church-planting endeavors of "high churches" and the more congregationally structured churches. He explained that "the Roman Catholic Church, the Oriental Orthodox Church, the Eastern Orthodox Church, and the Church of England respond to migration by extending the existing structure, whereas Protestantism reacts to it by creating full, new structures."[531] This latter approach has led to a greater growth pattern and multiplication cycle. He further added that migrant congregations were far more mission-minded and zealous for evangelism than were the established congregations.[532]

Studies were done exploring the relationship of geography to culture. In an article, John Leonard, professor of practical theology at Westminster Theological

Seminary, observed, "Because of globalization, speed of transport, and technology, distance is virtually irrelevant."[533] He expressed two results of separating culture from geography. The first is that immigrants do not have to leave their culture when they leave their homelands. Such immigrants continue to be mono-cultural while in their adopted land. They are also called "transnationals" or members of "communities that sit astride political borders and that, in a very real sense, are neither here nor there but in both places simultaneously."[534] The second result is that people can now identify with cultures and countries in which they have never lived.

By the conclusion of the 1990s, IMB workers embraced the strategic potential for starting churches among immigrants or large concentrations of ethnic groups. After many wars in former Yugoslavia, separate strategies were developed to reach diverse ethnic groups. Church planting among Croats in Bosnia needed a different strategy than starting a church among Bosnians.[535] Likewise, reaching many Hungarians in Romania prompted a different approach than the plan for engaging Romanians. Two conflicting realities emerged. On the one hand, sometimes immigrant families held on to their heritage more tightly as a defense mechanism in order to remain true to their homeland and familial practice. Conversely, some immigrant families more quickly embraced the practices, values, and even religious heritage of their adopted land.[536] IMB missionaries worked hard to discern the different tendencies and to wisely engage these unique populations.

In the late 1990s, IMB personnel were influencing the start of Russian-speaking churches in Latvia, Poland, and the Czech Republic.[537] Gary and Cathy Ramey were assigned to engage Russian speakers in the eastern part of Latvia and were catalytic in helping start many new groups. While the work among Latvians was stagnant, the work among the Russian speakers expanded and even influenced work among Russians in Lithuania. Several Russians and Ukrainians attended a Bible study in Prague, Czech Republic, after the turn of the century. Several came to faith and soon started a group, which grew into a Baptist church.

Many Romanian Baptist churches were started in Portugal, Spain, and Italy. These are some of the largest churches in the respective Baptist unions in those countries. IMB workers currently serve among Poles in England, Serbs in Bosnia, Albanians in Macedonia, and other immigrant populations from Eastern Europe.

## Reflections of entering a new region

Though forbidden to live in Eastern Europe for decades, IMB workers like John Allen Moore (1940s–1960s) and John David Hopper (1970s–1980s) related as closely as possible with Baptists cut off by the Iron Curtain.[538] Stories abound of the dangers of traveling into Eastern Europe as a tourist.

Hopper shared of the common practice of being followed by a KGB worker, multiple interrogations, and even a "sting operation" trying to place him in a compromising situation.[539] Yet Hopper "counted it all joy" to relate to the many unions in the former Soviet Union. He recalled with great excitement the

> Multitudes of American volunteers were rushing to experience the formerly communist "evil empire," and many wanted to meet personnel like Lozuk.

opening of 12 time zones and the unprecedented opportunity for the gospel to spread into a vast region. In his reflections, he argued that contact and coordination with the existing unions should have been stronger, and a less fragmented entrance would have better served the IMB.[540]

Raised in the home of Belarussian immigrants to America, George Lozuk never expected the day that the Soviet Union would open to Baptist missionaries. After three decades of faithful service in South America with the IMB, he and his wife, Veda Rae, were shocked to have the opportunity to move to Moscow as the first missionaries in the IMB's history to live in Russia.[541] He was the perfect pioneer to open the work in Russia. Multitudes of American volunteers were rushing to experience the formerly communist "evil empire," and many wanted to meet personnel like Lozuk. He was patient and always willing to help American volunteers who came to Russia, even those without relationship to the IMB.[542] Despite the challenges of a new setting for their final term of service, the Lozuks were instrumental in building good will with Russian Baptist leaders and opening the door for many missionaries to join them.

The reflections of Isam Ballenger included both joy and sadness. He rejoiced to see many Baptist leaders that he had befriended in his travels to Eastern Europe emerge into the new day of freedom. He also celebrated with them the opportunity to open or reopen training centers and many closed churches. But he also wrote that "the rapid changes caused many United States Christians' excitement to overwhelm their judgment. It happened at the IMB as well. There were a number of dynamics in play. The Europe office was already under deep suspicion by the trustees. There was no way we could move fast enough for them."[543] He felt that greater consultation with national leaders would have led to a smoother transition into the new region.

Applications are available for current and future world contexts. Though far from identical to the momentous changes of Eastern Europe in the late 1980s, some parts of the world are still closed to an open, missionary presence. Places like North Korea and the nations of North Africa stand out among these countries. The IMB is already actively working, either residentially or nonresidentially, to engage the peoples of these lands and is better prepared if the borders open in the future.

# 21

## SPECIFIC ISSUES IN TAKING DOWN A WALL

Geopolitical changes in Eastern Europe in the late 1980s were unprecedented. As a result, mission-sending organizations in the West did not have a tried-and-true blueprint to follow when the new freedoms came. The IMB rejoiced with the new opportunities and genuinely desired to enter the region with the best strategy of deployment, investment of resources, and steps of engagement for the work. As in most endeavors, some of the measures were extremely successful, some led to average results, and some failed to reach their desired goals.

### Opening work with transfers

One key decision made by the IMB as Eastern Europe opened to a missionary presence was the sending of transfers to open the work in each country. As noted earlier, the Steeles were an exception as they moved to Yugoslavia in 1988, though Nela Williams had already been living in the country for many years.[544] The argument was made that transfers could be deployed, adapt, and liaise with the hosting Baptist union more quickly. Ballenger reflected that "most of these transfers, perhaps all of these, did not gain proficiency in the language. Therefore, how effective were they?"[545] In early discussions with Baptist unions, the advantage of sending transfers was often mentioned to the national leaders. This was important because of the basic process of requesting new personnel. John Deal reported, "At the time I was there, the area office worked in cooperation with the unions and relied on them to submit requests for personnel or worked in consultation with the area office."[546]

Some job assignments written for transfer missionaries later opened up to new appointees.[547] Susie and I were appointed to serve in Poland in 1990 only after John Deal called the president of the Polish Baptist Union and received approval that new appointees could fill the church-planter assignment in Krakow, Poland. By 1993, most countries had been entered, and the prioritization of transfers was dropped. Some missionaries continued to transfer into the region, but these were largely treated the same as transfers anywhere in the world.

An evaluation of the effectiveness of the transfers is mixed. Accounting for the diverse and uncharted contexts into which they entered, many positive steps of service can be affirmed. Most workers effectively fulfilled their assignments of liaison with the national Baptist unions. As the IMB moved into a more aggressive stance regarding evangelism and church planting, some were ill equipped to transition into the new role. James aptly explained, "Strategies adopted by the IMB at this time required significant changes in strategies throughout the world and impacted strategy in Europe in a significant way. A large number of remaining missionaries throughout Europe were divided not only in their loyalty to the IMB but seriously questioned the current directions in strategy."[548] The strength of having previous experience with the IMB sometimes became a negative for a transfer who often longed for the "old way" they used to do things.

A subset of transfers should be noted. In a few very specialized situations, transfers were urged to "seize the moment" in an extraordinary time of need for general evangelists or humanitarian work. The situation in Bosnia following the brutal years of war was such an example. Six couples approaching their retirement moved to Bosnia to serve a final term of two to four years in order to help with some humanitarian assistance and to start new Bible study groups.[549]

Few transfers reached a high level of proficiency in the language. The general nature of their role often provided a rationale since they spent most of their time meeting with union leadership and working under their strategy. Expectations in the pioneer area of church planting were low or nonexistent and often very difficult, so most gravitated away from such initiatives. A final impacting influence relates to the longevity of the transfers. Due to many factors, like age and effectiveness, over 80 percent of the transfers served only a single term in Eastern Europe.

## Opening with fraternal representatives or highlighting the Baptist Union vision

Another calculated decision was entering each new country with a liaison missionary, generally called a fraternal representative. This designation provided a broad enough job title for the workers to largely serve under the direction and strategy of a hosting Baptist union. This pattern had some historic precedent in Western Europe so was consistent with the IMB beyond the borders of Eastern Europe.

The argument could also be made that the IMB had sent tens of thousands of dollars to support the ministries of the Eastern European Union during the 1970s and 1980s and therefore trusted their direction and strategies. Most of the leaders in these countries suffered for their faith and were highly esteemed as friends and brothers. The deployment of fraternal representatives was simply the next step to continue the encouragement of the existing and future work.

This deployment strategy decision reflected a deep, philosophical position in the IMB in the 1980s. In many ways, such a deployment into the new countries was a logical step in that historical context. Parks, Ballenger, and Parker often reiterated that the national unions were the initiators of strategy, and the IMB personnel were supporters, enablers, and encouragers. Reflecting on the strength of the IMB entrance into Eastern Europe, John Deal said, "The positives were that personnel worked in partnership with unions as they had in the past."[550] This philosophical conviction was possibly the greatest issue that prompted the resignations of all four of these leaders.

Parks's successor, Jerry Rankin, recalled the initial days of the demise of the Soviet Union and the IMB's response: "Dr. Parks continually explained that we can only respond to requests from national Baptist leaders, and we were still waiting for them to determine what they wanted us to do. I thought that was atrocious—we sat on our hands and could not take initiative and could do only what the Baptist Convention requested. That set us back several years."[551] This response clearly reflects the transition that occurred at the IMB and the clear shift in strategic deployments and initiatives.

To evaluate the deployment of fraternal representatives as a failure is not completely fair or accurate. In some countries where unions had aggressive church-planting strategies, like Ukraine and Moldova, these workers had great potential for impact and effectiveness. Also it is unfair to criticize personnel for fulfilling the tasks to which they were assigned, even if history may deem those ministries as less strategic or advancing. The climate of the IMB changed drastically in the 1990s, so a repeat of such a strategy step is not likely in the immediate future.

## Hesitancy for an aggressive response

A lesson interrelated to the previous two was the hesitancy or overly cautious response to the unexpected new day of the 1980s. An objective assessment regarding the speed of response or deployment is difficult, but IMB leaders expressed the desire to move deliberately and thoughtfully during those immediate days following the changes. Discussions between the IMB leadership and the trustees revealed different opinions regarding the manner and timing of response into Eastern Europe.

The first response to the fall of the Berlin Wall was the naming of a task force on European strategy. Meeting in January 1990, the members of the trustee group were Dale Cain (chairman), Gary Burden, Steve Hardy, Hoyt Savage, and David Stephen.[552] In their report, they defined their task as "to understand the European setting for cooperative evangelism through reviewing the strategies and policies of the past, present, and future as well as critically evaluating the findings in order to strengthen our evangelistic efforts in Europe." They purposed to hear from a broad representation of personnel, both on the field and in the United States. The chairman wrote to 38 missionaries in Europe for input, whether positive or negative, as well as for suggestions to enhance the evangelistic efforts in Europe. The trustees also said that they would be evaluating books and reports written by various authors, including missionaries Bill Wagner and Robert Cochran and Cal Guy, emeritus professor at Southwestern Seminary. All of this information, they stated, would help them make recommendations for improving the IMB's evangelistic efforts in Europe.[553]

The discussion continued at the following trustee meeting. The task force added that in Eastern Europe, "Accomplishments include the appointment of personnel to Hungary and a missionary for media work in Eastern Europe; also personnel requests have been received for Poland and the Soviet Union. Personnel of the East Europe Mission will continue deliberations with Baptist leaders of East European countries."[554]

From such records, it is easy to discern that the process was deliberate with high need for detailed clarification and agreement between all parties. A growing majority of trustees vocally argued against the report for a more aggressive entrance into the former Soviet Union. Leading pastors in the SBC and convention leaders also lobbied for an immediate widespread deployment into Eastern Europe. In a phone conversation with Ballenger, Morris Chapman, chief executive officer of the SBC, gave his opinion for a plan to evangelize the Soviet Union, which was also the predominant opinion of that day. "We should send 10 of our best SBC preachers to preach in stadiums in major cities of the USSR. We should ask the nationals to rent stadiums and plan crusades, lasting two weeks ... to accommodate our preachers' schedules. We should prepare literature to give to the people who answer the call to decision (a la Billy Graham)."[555]

Such strategies, although well meaning, revealed a shortsighted and overly simplistic understanding of the context in Eastern Europe. Since the atmosphere of the IMB Board of Trustees was unhealthy and suspicious during these deliberations, this context greatly impacted communication and tangible steps forward. Unfortunately, the relationship that developed between IMB leadership and the trustees, especially as it related to the needed response in Eastern Europe, was untrusting.[556] The power struggle continued into the 1990s, and a strong, clear, and visionary deployment of personnel never was implemented.

An early traveler into Eastern Europe after the borders opened was Larry Cox, who had previously served with the IMB but joined the staff of Mississippi College in the late 1980s. He set up educational projects, which helped facilitate the arrival of some missionaries into the former Soviet Union. He recalled,

"We missed opportunities by not being ready to mobilize enough people to go to serve."

"The greatest weakness was the response of the IMB and Southern Baptists. We missed opportunities by not being ready to mobilize enough people to go to serve."[557] The Lord later led Cox to give leadership, under John Floyd, as the strategy associate for Central Europe.

By the middle of the 1990s, the IMB had yet to deploy personnel to several countries, including Lithuania, Georgia, and Armenia. Lithuania and Georgia were entered by new appointees in 1996, and Armenia was opened by transfers in 1999.[558] None of these had the title of fraternal representative but entered as church planters.

The deployment process improved in the IMB in the mid-1990s, and the rise of nonresidential missionaries helped prepare some future workers to enter new countries that would open. These missionaries would study the language and culture and were ready to enter when the borders were relaxed. The implementation of "New Directions" addressed this hesitancy and replaced it with a bolder and more aggressive stance toward new opportunities.[559]

## Large turnover of personnel

One of the most painful lessons of the 1990s was the negative impact of attrition among missionaries. Especially challenging was the loss of basically all experienced senior leadership in Eastern Europe. Less than 20 percent of the missionaries who transferred to Eastern Europe between 1990 and 1996 stayed beyond one term of service.[560] Though exact statistics are difficult to compile, the best research shows that about one-third retired after their term, about one-third transferred to a different field, and about one-third resigned. The high number of retirees can be defended with the widespread call for missionaries to consider concluding their service with the IMB in an assignment in Eastern Europe. These mature servants should be commended for their willingness to move to a new culture with a difficult language.

The large numbers of subsequent transfers and resignations are more difficult to interpret. The Wardlaws were denied visa extensions, which left transfer as the only option besides resignation.[561] No other transfer left because of the inability to secure legal status in their country. At least one transfer returned to their previous field of service, and one was asked to take a leadership role in the newly developed Central and Eastern Europe region, which prompted a move to Germany.[562]

The relatively large number of resignations and transfers is difficult to document statistically. Whenever a missionary resigns from service with the IMB, he fills out a brief survey giving his reason or reasons for the step. Of course, these reasons are confidential, and only large compilations are available to leadership in the IMB. Through various discussions with former missionaries in Eastern Europe, I discovered three basic categories for the majority of the resignations.

Some resigned out of frustration or disagreement with the IMB. Some of this related to the new emphasis on evangelism and the movement away from a support role to national Baptist unions. Thirty-three missionaries resigned from Eastern Europe from 1991 to 1993, including all of the IMB leaders in Europe.[563] These changes did not greatly affect new missionaries who had never worked under the old system.

A second major influence that prompted resignation was the difficult living and working conditions in the former Soviet Union. The first workers into the countries testified to food shortages, power outages, and harsh living conditions. Dan Panter commented that "the economy was still the old Soviet system, and everything was scarce but cheap."[564] "Brown outs" were common and oftentimes services, like running water, were scheduled for only certain hours each day.[565] Fairly simple tasks like paying a phone bill or registering a car could take a whole day or more. Some also testified to the strain of the culture and sometimes repressive measures of the government. Bob Tucker remembered that his "phone was tapped," which prompted continual diligence in his communication.[566] Policemen often stopped cars without cause, insisting upon a bribe.

The third category for resignation was a combination of many factors like children's needs, aging parents, health needs, and the other general reasons often given for resignation from the IMB. The combination of these many factors contributed to a greater-than-normal turnover of personnel and delayed the effective service in many of the countries for several years. In fact, some countries, like Belarus, Slovakia, and Moldova, did not welcome a second-term missionary for over a decade after the first IMB workers arrived.

The obvious result of such attrition is the lack of continuity and the skepticism that may grow in the hearts of the national Baptist leaders. Most missionaries spoke loudly of their intention to stay long term to serve with nationals for many years only to resign after a three- or four-year term. Buck Burch, arriving in Russia in

1998, said, "From 1992 to 1998, the personnel that made up IMB in Russia had been almost totally replaced by a new set. Therefore, those who were at work in Russia in 2000 spoke very little Russian and were not capable of leading small groups themselves."[567] Lee Bradley, in Albania, believed missionaries had to invest more than seven years to see a church take root and grow.[568]

Diverse factors contributed to the large turnover of personnel in the early engagement years in Eastern Europe. Some attrition was actually the result of strategy highlighting the deployment of mature missionaries nearing retirement. Though the decision to resign is hard to predict, this lesson should be considered as potential candidates are interviewed about opening new work or new countries.

## Lack of adequate preparation for workers

The high attrition rate in Eastern Europe exposed a fundamental challenge of adequate preparation for missionaries who deployed to the region. Most transfers had served with the IMB at least two terms before moving to Eastern Europe so had been removed from their Richmond-based training of four to six weeks for many years. Most received some basic field orientation of up to a week, and many were introduced to the national leadership upon their arrival to their new country. Beyond that orientation, additional training was almost nonexistent.

> Because the world was changing at a startling rate politically, morally, and spiritually, [the trustees] were concerned that it would be harder to find quality candidates available for appointment.

The training process for new IMB missionaries was being improved, but no one had experience serving in Eastern Europe; specialized preparation was not available to the new appointees. The trustees' discussion at the April 1990 meeting revealed an interesting concern. Because the world was changing at a startling rate politically, morally, and spiritually, they were concerned that it would be harder to find quality candidates available for appointment.[569] Prior to "New Directions," a master's degree was the general expectation for career missionaries as was a minimum of two years of experience on a church staff. Some of these requirements were relaxed in the late 1990s, and candidates from a broader background were appointed to overseas service.

The challenges in Eastern Europe were unique, and the trustee task force discussed the many differences compared with the work in the United States. The task force reported, "We acknowledge that some excellent tools exist for evangelism training, notably, *Continuing Witness Training* and *Evangelism Explosion*. We are aware that these tools do not always adapt to European culture with the same success they enjoy in American churches. The incarnational approach to missions is, therefore, reaffirmed by our task force."[570] The task force made two accurate and related conclusions related to the priority training needs in Europe. They concluded that, "One deficiency revealed during our study is the area of developing strategy for urban evangelization."[571] They suggested that another task force be created to study the need for greater creativity and effectiveness in reaching the major cities. The second strong proposal was made to the personnel selection department that "whenever possible, candidates should be encouraged to develop some experience in church planting before moving to the field."[572] Unfortunately, few IMB missionaries deployed to Eastern Europe in the first decade of openness had church-planting experience in the States prior to appointment.

As the IMB grew in its emphasis of church planting throughout the 1990s, the training provided for new personnel was sharpened in this area. Yet, receiving training and having experience were two different things. Burch reported on this reality among the workers in Russia. He wrote, "Of all of the IMB missionaries who have been appointed to Russia, I know of only one who has ever come with any church-planting experience prior to arrival. (Interestingly, this person is not on a church-planting team but works in the business office). When we arrived, Russian

Baptists' senior pastors looked for two things from us: money for more church buildings, which they soon discovered we could not provide, and church-planting expertise, which they also discovered we did not have."[573] The combination of limited experience in urban church planting coupled with the unprecedented and unknown context of 12 time zones emerging from communism exposed the challenge of adequately preparing a workforce to tackle the new target. Less than ideal results can be criticized, or they can be marveled at because progress was made regardless.

## Peril of subsidies

The peril of subsidies is also referred to as the pitfall of dependence or may even be framed as the challenge of volunteers. The topics of subsidies and volunteers do not always go hand in hand, but often they are related. After decades of providing large sums of money to national Baptist unions, the IMB learned that such subsidies can harm long-term work. Drastic adjustments were made in the structural changes of "New Directions." This major shift from sponsoring national institutions and projects to concentrating on pioneer church planting was met with resistance by some national leaders. Their quick fix was to see volunteers as the source for continued, or possibly new, funding for projects.

Whether from the IMB budget or gifts from volunteers, nearby pastors often responded with jealousy at the discrepancy between his salary or church budget and the salary or project funds available to the sponsored church. Panter discovered that subsidies often turned many hearts away from the work of the gospel.[574] In economies emerging slowly from the shadow of communism, new sources of wealth were quickly embraced and values often lost in the transaction. Potential church planters would sometimes wait idly for a "sponsor" instead of stepping out by faith or working bivocationally, as many of his national brethren did for half a century.

A couple of years after becoming president of the IMB, Jerry Rankin toured many of the countries of Eastern Europe, meeting with union leaders and missionaries. He found that although volunteers had been effective, the "enthusiasm for immediate results had established a debilitating pattern of subsidy." This dependence on behalf of nationals had deprived them of a faith that would recognize God's resources to meet needs. He continued that after WWI, the IMB "learned the tragic lesson that building churches and paying pastors did not produce sustainable, indigenous growth. It would be most unfortunate if we did not learn from those experiences and the painful process of trying to break off dependency on foreign resources."[575]

Thousands of well-meaning volunteers flooded into Eastern Europe with the genuine desire of sharing Christ. Some arrived with little or no training and were intent on using American-style evangelism or church methods. Many saw poverty or small churches longing for better facilities and quickly pledged support for the pastor and the new church building. Such steps were taken with right motives but often hindered the long-term work of the pastor and the church. The lesson of subsidy is a lesson that must be retaught and relearned by every generation of missionary and every location of mission work.

## Perceptions of the IMB

The final challenging lesson relates to the perception of the IMB in Europe from the early 1990s to the present. Divergent factors contributed to the changing practice and focus of the IMB. The "70/30 Plan" of 1988 formalized a steady movement toward greater intentionality in evangelism and church planting. The decision to defund the International Baptist Theological Seminary in Ruschlikon due to theological differences with IMB trustees had grave consequences among the leaders of the EBF and many Baptist unions. Although the Hamburg Agreement was a positive step forward after this defunding, most European leaders were still wary and uncertain about the future working relationship with the IMB. Not long after the meeting in Hamburg, the IMB restructured its organization and removed the position of area vice presidents, so Sam James no longer related to the European leaders after 1993. This was a setback to some of the positive momentum.

As relationships began to improve with examples of fruitful services in some countries, the IMB announced "New Directions" in 1997. Many national leaders felt that unilateral decisions were made and that their traditional strategies and needs were no longer important to the IMB. This perception continued for many years. About a decade after the Hamburg Agreement, the Southern Baptist Convention voted to break ties with the Baptist World Alliance.[576] Although the IMB never had official "ties" with the BWA, many European union leaders used the occasion to attack the SBC and often the IMB.[577]

These controversial events underscore the constant challenge of relating to various partners and working constantly to keep the focus of evangelism and church planting in the middle of each discussion. The IMB is again slowly regaining acceptance by many Baptist unions in Eastern Europe but will need to be diligent to serve effectively and humbly in the countries where they minister.

# 22

## HOW WE'LL GET THROUGH THE WALL

As they say, "Hindsight is better than foresight." As we learn from our mistakes, we must also look at what the IMB got right in the past 100 years in Eastern Europe. So what did we get right? Here's my take on what we can learn from the successes.

### Encouragement through presence

National leaders and Baptist partners often affirmed that one of the greatest results of the early work of missionaries was the simple fact of their presence.[578] Long denied contact with believers from the West, nationals were often starved for contact with brethren in the free nations. The fellowship of the gospel is precious, especially when denied for decades.

Despite many obstacles, our pioneer missionaries, the Gills, persevered for years to build and maintain strong relationships among the European brethren. Not only a presence, Gill was a great advocate for Eastern Europe, keeping the work on the minds of Southern Baptists. With this *koinonia*, or intimate participation, having been developed, an atmosphere was created for other missionaries to be accepted and loved. In one of Everett Gill's report to trustees after a brief trip to

Yugoslavia, he said, "During the war years, there has been decided growth. About 200 members have been baptized into the churches yearly. The brethren long for the return of Dr. and Mrs. John Allen Moore and the reopening of the seminary."[579] Decades would pass before missionaries would arrive again to settle in Yugoslavia. That longing for coworkers only strengthened with the passing of time and the worsening of conditions in the Soviet Union.

In Belarus, Dan Panter summarized, "I believe our greatest impact was PRESENCE among them as we joined our resources to theirs and began to labor together. We, Americans and Belarusians, found we had a common passion to serve our Lord and with understanding and patience, we could work well together."[580] In Latvia, the turnover of IMB missionaries was even more pronounced than in many countries, and the Union was hesitant to invest in a relationship with the new IMB workers. The Erwins arrived in 1996 and dedicated the first two years to language learning. By 1998, other IMB families working among Latvians had retired or resigned. The Union asked Erwin to teach in the seminary and though that was not his assignment, he agreed and helped rebuild trust with the Union. He was then able to influence a young church planter to start a church in a Riga suburb. His presence in the seminary was a positive example of cooperation and was valued as highly by the Union as the birth of a new church.[581]

The longest and greatest example of presence in the past 100 years was the exemplary service of Nela Williams. We can practically say that she has lived and ministered in Yugoslavia her whole life, even after the death of her husband. Nela faithfully taught Greek at the small seminary in Yugoslavia and still consistently shares God's love in this beloved home, although retired. For three terms, she was the only IMB presence in Eastern Europe. She is dearly loved by colleagues and nationals alike.[582]

## Cooperation and influence with Baptist unions

Though there were challenging relationships between the IMB and European Baptist leaders, the amazing truth is that the IMB was extremely influential among many national partners. Sometimes the influence came as a connector to Baptist state conventions or other partner opportunities. Sometimes the influence came through training and educational assignments filled by IMB personnel. Still other times, a direct influence was seen in vision casting and church planting.

Some Baptist leaders still affirmed the essential role played by the IMB and state convention partnerships with the national unions during the early 1990s. In Hungary, a partnership with Virginia Baptists accelerated the expansion of some existing churches and the establishment of a union campground.[583] In Poland, the Baptist Union signed a cooperative agreement with the convention of North Carolina, which resulted in the building of the Polish Baptist Theological Seminary. The retired president

> "Your people have bought apartments and learned the language, and we know you are here to stay and work with us."

of the Polish Baptist Union wrote, "The partnership with the North Carolina Baptist Convention was wonderful. There were only positive points. Thanks to them, we were able to complete the seminary complex in the Radosc suburb of Warsaw."[584] Many other unions benefited from state partnerships brokered by the IMB missionaries.

On his trip to Eastern Europe in 1996, Jerry Rankin discovered that the Baptist unions would work with most anyone, but leaders reiterated to him that "your people have bought apartments and learned the language, and we know you are here to stay and work with us."[585] One of the union leaders who met with Rankin during that trip was Gregory Kommendant, president of the Baptist Union of Ukraine. He already saw the positive influence of the early workers and asked the IMB to send 120 additional missionaries with the desire to send two church planters into every district of the country.[586] When asked about the early influence of the IMB in Ukraine, Kommendant gave a positive response to their previous experience with the IMB.[587]

A full assessment of IMB workers' influence in Eastern Europe is impossible, but evidence exists throughout the vast region in the form of training materials, Bible study methods, small group models, and multiplied young "Timothys" now leading churches and sometimes leading unions.

## Perseverance of personnel

I've mentioned the Gills and Nela Williams, but there are workers in the past 20 years who have shown the same kind of perseverance. In countries where workers have remained beyond two terms, more widespread and longer lasting fruit is evident.

One example is the Magalhaes family. For over 15 years, coming as a young couple, they have continued to follow God's call in Lithuania. Church planting was nonexistent in the country when they arrived, and no viable partners were present to help with the work. Though isolated and working in a country without an encouraging Baptist Union, they invested in learning the language and culture. Their children attended national schools into their teens, and their family persisted during the slow, painstaking steps that church planting requires. In a country with five Baptist churches when they arrived, they have seen the birth of three vibrant congregations in their years of service.[588]

The IMB family that opened the work in Armenia in 1999 was unable to live within the country for several years, so they faithfully targeted their people group from an adjacent country. New Armenian believers traveled to the workers to receive training and return to their country. After enduring this separation for eight years, the family was able to enter the country and accelerate the work.[589]

Lee Bradley arrived in Albania as a journeyman in 1996, only to evacuate during the Albanian civil war in 1997.[590] He later returned to Albania as a career missionary and has led the work there for over a decade. He started a couple of churches as well as a training center to equip Albanian believers to start churches. He affirmed strategically that "the places where missionaries have invested seven to 10 years are the places where the churches have taken root and grown."[591] He has proven his own conviction with his endurance.

Another family deployed to work among Russians in a partially closed country in the 1990s faced many challenges in their work. They learned Russian, led several people to faith, and provided basic training for them. The wife was diagnosed with cancer, and the couple returned to the States for treatment. After two years, the cancer was deemed incurable but could be arrested. She had the prognosis of a long life. She would have to follow a strict regimen, which included special doses of medicine. The couple immediately contacted the IMB requesting permission to return to their city of assignment. The medical department was hesitant to grant medical approval because of the uncertainty of medical care, availability of the special medicine, and the long-range effects of living in that environment. The leadership of the region met with the couple and the medical department in Richmond to discuss their redeployment. The wife bluntly asked, "Why can we not go back and continue to tell the people about Jesus?" The medical doctor responded, "Because you may not get appropriate medical attention and could die." She quickly responded, "We are all going to die, why can't I do so while serving the Lord?" They returned to the field and are still engaging Russians with the gospel.[592]

These examples are representative of scores of faithful missionaries who have served through extremely difficult times. They have seen many colleagues come and go and have endured. Many work in frigid climates among unresponsive peoples, yet remain faithful. One of the greatest lessons to celebrate in Eastern Europe over the past 20 years is that the Lord blesses perseverance. When Nela was asked for her advice to new missionaries, she said, "If you are genuinely called of God, you'll face the challenges and persevere. You must stand on the call. Things rock and change, but you can take anything when you're firmly planted in God's call and His help. Circumstances changed for me, but my call and God didn't."[593]

## Cultural adaptation of personnel

One lesson, which every generation must learn, is the high value of cultural adaptation of missionaries. The IMB work in Eastern Europe stands on the shoulders of such examples like John Allen Moore and John David Hopper.[594] Both of these men were known for their cultural sensitivity and their determination to learn the language of their host countries. The combination of humility and hard work opened doors of influence that lasted over half a century when combined. Isam Ballenger said, "I place so much value on language learning as a basic necessity for effective missionary service."[595]

Many of the first missionaries in the former Soviet Union did not have the opportunity to become fluent in the language. George Lozuk was an exception to this reality due to his childhood in a Russian-speaking home.[596] The Russian Baptist Union's surprise at his fluency coupled with their respect for age combined to form the perfect setting for his strong influence in the early days.

In Ukraine, families like the Stockwells, Byrds, Rays, and Fords blazed the trail of effective cultural adaptation and influence. The Stockwells, along with their three sons, worked together in Kharkov to establish a church-planting center and to work catalytically among nationals. From the very beginning, they worked with new church plants led by nationals. He said, "We walked alongside nationals to provide events that would draw the lost to the churches and to open doors into the community."[597] Similarly the Rays, along with their two daughters, have lived among the Ukrainians and have been accepted as leaders and partners.

National leaders often have commented on the difference between the missionaries who leave their homes to "enter the mission field" and those who open their homes and actually live in the field. Many times the children attend national schools, and missionary families vacation with national friends. Our middle daughter, Meredith, even won a spelling bee in the Polish national school where she attended. Many missionaries in Eastern Europe have heard a variation of one of the greatest statements of affirmation afforded to international workers: "You are one of us."

## Strategies related to deployment

The practical task of deploying personnel into Eastern Europe was overwhelming. To open a map of Eastern Europe and see the largest country in the world along with over 20 nearby countries was a daunting challenge. The numerous Baptist unions involved and the varied perceived needs made the creation of a uniformed, deployment strategy difficult.

Ballenger recalled early conversations with Baptist leaders at a meeting in Budapest, Hungary, and the numerous distinct agendas. He reported that the Hungarian leaders wanted to decide where IMB personnel would serve and preferred that the missionaries not be church planters.[598] The Romanians were "quite confusing" as one leading pastor asked for funds to help set up a rival seminary to the official Baptist seminary in Bucharest.[599] Both seminaries wanted IMB personnel and support.

The first wave of missionaries, and especially the fraternal representatives, tended to locate in the capital cities. This was logical since their assignment was intertwined with the work of the sponsoring Baptist union. Usually within a year of arrival, the fraternal representative started writing job requests for future workers. Many of these requests were for church planters, but different unions had different approaches to their placement. Some unions, as well as IMB workers, took the "paint-the-map" approach where new workers were assigned to unreached and often isolated large cities. These workers were assigned geographically throughout a country according to population and unreached statistics. A union may highlight the top 10 cities that needed engagement and send the next 10 families into these cities. Some difficult lessons were learned from this approach. One lesson related to the type of missionary that was needed to initiate new work in a large city. Most newly appointed missionaries arrived with no church-planting experience and were often ill equipped to tackle the intimidating task of starting new work. Within four or five years, the IMB leadership in Europe realized that few of these pioneer families were thriving in their assignments. A major reason for this reality led to the second lesson that isolation was more of a factor in effective deployment than first thought. The success rate of isolated families in the major cities of Eastern Europe was small. These realities led to a more effective plan of deployment.

> The success rate of isolated families in the major cities of Eastern Europe was small.

The timing of the lessons was fortuitous as "New Directions" arrived. One key element in the new vision was that missionaries would serve together on teams.[600] The mutual accountability and support proved essential as teams served longer with a greater impact after the changes. One key to the team's effectiveness was the conscious effort to incorporate non-IMB team members to further the work, train more workers, and expand into new teams and new locations.

Some countries, like Ukraine and Poland, developed a strong system of consultation in the deployment of new personnel. Ukrainian leaders periodically met with IMB leaders in the country to plan a year or two ahead of the next worker's arrival. Stockwell summarized the positive relationship: "The Baptist Union has been strongly influenced in the areas of church planting and cross-cultural missionary sending by IMB personnel. Our personnel have always been invited to 'sit at the table' for discussions for developing vision and strategy for the future."[601] In Poland, IMB leaders would consult with the Baptist leaders to prayerfully choose the next two to three cities that needed church planters before writing the requests.

Strong lessons regarding strategic deployment of personnel resulted from the first decade of work in the former Soviet Union. Consultation with unions, when they exist, is preferred, and deployment as teams gives greater effectiveness and longevity. These lessons transcend geographical and cultural particulars.

## Can the remaining wall be broken, once for all?

With all the progress that has been made, can the wall that remains be completely removed? Absolutely. We know that one day, representatives of all people groups will be present at the feet of Jesus, worshipping Him eternally. The IMB's current vision statement is: "Our vision is a multitude from every language, people, tribe, and nation knowing and worshipping our Lord Jesus Christ."[602] We are more passionate than ever about starting churches, especially in unengaged, unreached people groups. Effective training is given to all missionaries related to starting reproducing groups and praying toward church-planting movements where churches will grow exponentially throughout a population segment.

The IMB intends to continue to deploy God-called men and women to Eastern Europe where over 98 percent of the population is still without hope in Christ Jesus.[603] It is a land filled with thousands of years of history where barriers to the gospel still exist. But it is also a place where people groups are finding hope through the gospel of Christ. It will take the power of God, desperate prayer, and partnership—IMB, other Great Commission groups, nationals, Baptist unions, and SBC churches—to see God's plan for the nations fulfilled. As faithful apostolic workers learn from the past and passionately pursue God's agenda for the future, the wall that remains will be shattered, and the vision of Revelation will be a reality.

# Acknowledgments

After preaching a crusade in Poland in 1990 and moving my family there to live in 1991, I met some of the Lord's choicest unsung heroes. At my insistence, we had numerous late-night conversations around the kitchen table about the hardships of communism, and they always responded with a shrug and explanation, "The Bible says to expect persecution." Our first Polish tutor, Krzysztof Bednarczyk, was a retired pastor, a lifelong learner, and encourager to us. Our first Polish pastor, Gustaw Cieslar, continues to be a dear friend and encourager. I give thanks to them, hundreds of other faithful Polish friends, and thousands of faithful believers throughout the former Soviet Union who persevered through hard times.

I also express thanks to the hundreds of American Christians over the past 20 years who have encouraged me to write a book recording our experiences and the history that we witnessed in the former Soviet Union.

Thanks go to Southeastern Baptist Theological Seminary for allowing me to research and write this book in the context of a Ph.D. program. Special thanks go to Al James, Joseph Solc, Bruce Ashford, Andreas Kostenberger, and Danny Akin.

I also appreciate the additional research of Bev Hollins, design work of Jana Owens, publishing support of Dan Allen, and the creative editing of Kim Davis.

Finally, thank you to the many faithful IMB missionaries who served throughout Eastern Europe from the 1920s to the present. I am grateful to the 100 or more former and present missionaries who agreed to be interviewed in preparation for this book. Of special note is Nela Williams, who alone served behind the "Iron Curtain" for many years and recently retired after 35 years of service; and Pauline Moore, who at 100 years of age is our only living tie to the great work in pre-WWII Eastern Europe.

## Soli Deo Gloria!

# APPENDIX 1

IMB APPOINTMENTS TO EASTERN EUROPE
## 1988–2000

| YEARS | TOTAL |
|---|---:|
| 1988 | 8 |
| 1989 | 3 |
| 1990 | 25 |
| 1991 | 50 |
| 1992 | 45 |
| 1993 | 54 |
| 1994 | 87 |
| 1995 | 72 |
| 1996 | 68 |
| 1997 | 68 |
| 1998 | 95 |
| 1999 | 120 |
| 2000 | 51 |
| GRAND TOTAL | 746 |

# APPENDIX 2

## Central and Eastern Europe Region Annual Statistical Reports 1988–2000

| Indicators | 1988 | 1989 | 1990 | 1991 | 1992 | 1993 | 1994 | 1995 | 1996 | 1997 | 1998 | 1999 | 2000 |
|---|---|---|---|---|---|---|---|---|---|---|---|---|---|
| Baptisms | 39 | 29 | 26 | 81 | 21,245 | 20,960 | 26,459 | 22,616 | 22,463 | 20,748 | 22,360 | 21,574 | 5,011 |
| Baptist Partner Home Missionaries | | | 2 | 22 | 226 | 55 | 40 | 236 | 252 | 587 | 2,536 | 1,224 | 741 |
| Baptist Partner International Missionaries | 1 | | | 3 | 4 | 2 | 2 | 50 | 31 | 9 | 434 | 566 | 420 |
| Church Members in Discipleship | 6 | 7 | | | 9,250 | 123 | 28,875 | 29,019 | 30,114 | 1,010 | 31,359 | 34,269 | 35,311 |
| Church Membership | 998 | 1,075 | 1,016 | 4,221 | 321,829 | 345,559 | 356,497 | 378,898 | 378,869 | 348,914 | 407,499 | 393,196 | 282,987 |
| Churches | 12 | 13 | 13 | 82 | 3,909 | 4,783 | 4,370 | 5,048 | 5,144 | 5,549 | 6,200 | 6,478 | 5,014 |
| New Believers in Discipleship | | | | | | | | | | | | | 3,505 |
| New Churches | | | | | | 372 | 313 | 551 | 295 | 292 | 316 | 398 | 133 |
| New Outreach Groups | | | | | | | | | | | | | 331 |
| Non-Residential Leadership Training | | | | | 486 | 2,235 | 1,298 | 508 | 447 | 235 | 7,320 | 8,094 | 7,588 |
| Participants in Church Bible Teaching | 619 | 691 | 653 | 812 | 84,705 | 159,839 | 252,275 | 249,516 | 251,374 | 65,897 | 178,194 | 190,454 | 180,893 |
| Residential Leadership Training | | | | | 517 | 784 | 631 | 1,298 | 1,404 | 1,237 | 4,391 | 4,068 | 3,482 |
| Total Outreach Groups | 14 | 15 | 13 | 42 | 711 | 847 | 994 | 1,997 | 2,327 | 1,413 | 1,353 | 1,210 | 677 |

# APPENDIX 3

## Central and Eastern Europe Region Annual Statistical Reports 2000–2008

| Indicators | 2000 | 2001 | 2002 | 2003 | 2004 | 2005 | 2006 | 2007 | 2008 |
|---|---|---|---|---|---|---|---|---|---|
| Baptisms | 5,011 | 17,690 | 25,607 | 19,830 | 22,078 | 21,100 | 23,576 | 19,174 | 19,103 |
| Baptist Partner Home Missionaries | 741 | 765 | 644 | 832 | 1,252 | 1,474 | 1,129 | 759 | 695 |
| Baptist Partner International Missionaries | 420 | 302 | 406 | 474 | 516 | 467 | 505 | 476 | 486 |
| Church Members in Discipleship | 35,311 | 35,375 | 48,813 | 50,455 | 38,527 | 44,118 | 42,131 | 49,264 | 49,246 |
| Church Membership | 282,987 | 325,016 | 483,589 | 494,916 | 516,755 | 499,547 | 518,422 | 478,762 | 479,234 |
| Churches | 5,014 | 5,286 | 8,028 | 8,391 | 8,241 | 8,594 | 8,877 | 7,946 | 8,106 |
| New Believers in Discipleship | 3,505 | 10,127 | 15,282 | 14,416 | 16,110 | 19,589 | 20,360 | 18,355 | 17,909 |
| New Churches | 133 | 365 | 475 | 329 | 421 | 324 | 307 | 276 | 233 |
| New Outreach Groups | 331 | 170 | 478 | 492 | 1,039 | 460 | 554 | 718 | 706 |
| Non-Residential Leadership Training | 7,588 | 8,099 | 5,378 | 6,371 | 7,409 | 7,449 | 9,861 | 11,411 | 12,458 |
| Participants in Church Bible Teaching | 180,893 | 184,904 | 138,318 | 158,984 | 160,900 | 162,214 | 188,707 | 195,676 | 192,723 |
| Residential Leadership Training | 3,482 | 4,833 | 3,587 | 3,611 | 5,124 | 4,159 | 3,634 | 3,685 | 4,261 |
| Total Outreach Groups | 677 | 878 | 1,659 | 1,998 | 4,106 | 3,797 | 2,990 | 3,304 | 3,552 |

# Notes

1. Everett Gill, letter to Dr. F. Love, December 22, 1921, archives.

2. J. C. Pollock, *The Faith of the Russian Evangelicals* (New York:McGraw-Hill, 1964), 57.

3. Ibid., 58.

4. Ibid., 62.

5. Walter Sawatsky, *Soviet Evangelicals Since World War II* (Scottdale, Pa.: Herald Press, 1981), 33.

6. Steve Durasoff, *The Russian Protestants: Evangelicals in the Soviet Union 1944-1964* (Rutherford, N.J.: Fairleigh Dickinson University Press, 1969), 42.

7. Ibid., 42.

8. Ibid., 39.

9. Ibid., 62. Oncken was born in Germany in 1800 and was very influential in the growth of Baptist missions in Europe.

10. Ibid., 133.

11. Sawatsky and Penner, *Mission,* 47.

12. Paul D. Steeves, "The Russian Baptist Union 1917–1935: Evangelical Awakening in Russia" (Ph.D. diss., University of Kansas, 1976), 37.

13. Sawatsky, *Soviet Evangelicals,* 35.

14. Durasoff, *The Russian Protestants,* 49.

15. Steeves, "The Russian Baptist Union," 53.

16. Ibid., 54.

17. Susan Wiley Hardwick, *Russian Refuge* (Chicago: University of Chicago Press, 1993), 36.

18. Sawatsky, *Soviet Evangelicals,* 36.

19. Ibid.

20. J. H. Rushbrooke, *Baptists in the USSR* (Nashville: Broadman, 1943), 8.

21. Sharyl Corrado and Toivo Pilli, eds., *Eastern European Baptist History: New Perspectives* (Prague: International Baptist Theological Seminary, 2007), 90.

22. Denton Lotz, ed., *Baptist Witness in the USSR* (Valley Forge, Pa.: International Ministries of the American Baptist Churches, USA, 1987), 27.

23. Rushbrooke, *Baptists in the USSR,* 9.

24. Corrado and Pilli, *Eastern European Baptist History,* 91.

25. Everett Gill, notes from Russian Baptist Publication, January 26, 1922, archives.

26. Ibid.

27. Ibid.

28. Ibid.

29. Ibid.

30. Ibid.

31. Ibid. The name given to the international sending arm of the Northern Baptist Convention (USA) in 1910.

32. Ibid.

33. Ibid. The convention formed in Philadelphia in 1851.

34. Ibid.

35. Ibid.

36. Minutes of the Foreign Mission Board of the SBC, Trustee Meeting, October 4, 1927, archives. The British Missionary Society was founded in 1792.

37. Minutes of the Foreign Mission Board of the SBC, Annual SBC Convention, May 17, 1922, archives.

38. Ibid.

39. J. D. Hughey, *Baptist Partnership in Europe* (Nashville: Broadman, 1982), 95.

40. Minutes of the Foreign Mission Board of the SBC, Annual SBC Convention, May 16, 1923, archives.

41. Minutes of the Foreign Mission Board of the SBC, Annual SBC Convention, May 17, 1922, archives.

42. Ibid.

43. Ibid.

44. Ibid.

45. Ibid.

46. Ibid.

47. Hughey, *Baptist Partnership,* 95.

48. Minutes of the Foreign Mission Board of the SBC, Annual SBC Convention, May 16, 1923, archives.

49. Ibid.

50. Minutes of the Foreign Mission Board of the SBC, Annual SBC Convention, May 9, 1929, archives.

51. Ibid.

52. Ibid.

53. Ibid.

54. Minutes of the Foreign Mission Board of the SBC, Trustee Meeting, October 2, 1929, archives.

55. Minutes of the Foreign Mission Board of the SBC, Annual SBC Convention, May 14, 1930, archives.

56. Minutes of the Foreign Mission Board of the SBC,

Annual SBC Convention, May 13, 1931, archives.

57. Ibid.

58. Minutes of the Foreign Mission Board of the SBC, Annual SBC Convention, May 13, 1932, archives.

59. Ibid.

60. Minutes of the Foreign Mission Board of the SBC, Annual SBC Convention, May 19, 1933, archives.

61. Ibid.

62. Ibid.

63. Minutes of the Foreign Mission Board of the SBC, Annual SBC Convention, May 13, 1937, archives.

64. Minutes of the Foreign Mission Board of the SBC, Annual SBC Convention, May 12, 1938, archives.

65. Minutes of the Foreign Mission Board of the SBC, Annual SBC Convention, May 17, 1939, archives.

66. Minutes of the Foreign Mission Board of the SBC, Trustee Meeting, December 15, 1939, archives.

67. Minutes of the Foreign Mission Board of the SBC, Annual SBC Convention, May 14, 1941, archives.

68. Minutes of the Foreign Mission Board of the SBC, Annual SBC Convention, June 12, 1940, archives.

69. Minutes of the Foreign Mission Board of the SBC, Annual SBC Convention, May 17, 1922, archives.

70. Ibid.

71. Minutes of the Foreign Mission Board of the SBC, Annual SBC Convention, May 16, 1923, archives.

72. Ibid.

73. Ibid.

74. Minutes of the Foreign Mission Board of the SBC, Annual SBC Convention, May 16, 1928, archives.

75. Ibid.

76. Ibid.

77. Minutes of the Foreign Mission Board of the SBC, Annual SBC Convention, May 13, 1931, archives.

78. Ibid.

79. Minutes of the Foreign Mission Board of the SBC, Trustee Meeting, October 21, 1936, archives.

80. Minutes of the Foreign Mission Board of the SBC, Annual SBC Convention, May 13, 1939, archives.

81. Minutes of the Foreign Mission Board of the SBC, Trustee Meeting, October 21, 1936, archives.

82. Ibid.

83. Minutes of the Foreign Mission Board of the SBC, Annual SBC Convention, May 13, 1937, archives.

84. Minutes of the Foreign Mission Board of the SBC, Annual SBC Convention, May 17, 1939, archives.

85. Ibid.

86. Minutes of the Foreign Mission Board of the SBC, Annual SBC Convention, May 17, 1922, archives.

87. Minutes of the Foreign Mission Board of the SBC, Annual SBC Convention, May 16, 1923, archives.

88. Ibid.

89. Ibid.

90. Ibid.

91. Minutes of the Foreign Mission Board of the SBC, Annual SBC Convention, May 16, 1928, archives.

92. Minutes of the Foreign Mission Board of the SBC, Annual SBC Convention, May 14, 1930, archives.

93. Minutes of the Foreign Mission Board of the SBC, Annual SBC Convention, May 13, 1932, archives.

94. Minutes of the Foreign Mission Board of the SBC, Annual SBC Convention, May 16, 1934, archives.

95. Ibid.

96. Ibid.

97. Minutes of the Foreign Mission Board of the SBC, Trustee Meeting, October 16, 1934, archives.

98. Minutes of the Foreign Mission Board of the SBC, Annual SBC Convention, May 16, 1939, archives.

99. Minutes of the Foreign Mission Board of the SBC, Annual SBC Convention, June 12, 1940, archives.

100. Ibid.

101. Nela Williams Mayer, interviewed by editor, 22 April 2012.

102. Pollock, The Faith, 82.

103. Ibid., 83.

104. Steeves, "The Russian Baptist Union," 253.

105. Ibid., 256.

106. Ibid., 245.

107. Pollock, The Faith, 83.

108. Hans Brandenburg, The Meek and the Mighty (New York: Oxford University Press, 1977), 191.

109. John L. McKenzie, The Roman Catholic Church (Garden City, N.Y.: Image Books, 1971), 13.

110. Ibid., 175–226.

111. Ibid., 165.

112. Ibid.

113. "The Universal Visible Church," n.p. [cited 11 November 2010]. Online: http://www .nonprotestantbaptists.com.

114. "The Universal Visible Church," n.p.

115. Lindsay Jones, ed., Encyclopedia of Religion. Vol. 3 (New York: Thomson Gale, 2005), 2114.

116. Thomas Corbishley, Roman Catholicism (New York: Harper, 1964), 72.

117. Hilaire Belloc, *Europe and the Faith* (London: Constable and Company, 1924), 5.

118. Ibid., 319.

119. Ibid., 330–31.

120. D. S. Roberts, *Islam: A Concise Introduction* (New York: Harper & Row, 1981), 5.

121. Patrick Sookhdeo, *A Christian's Pocket Guide to Islam* (Fearn, Scotland: Christian Focus Publications, 2001), 10.

122. Roberts, *Islam,* 5.

123. F. E. Peters, *A Reader on Classical Islam* (Princeton, N.J.: Princeton University Press, 1994), xv.

124. Roberts, *Islam,* 36.

125. Ibid., 36–39.

126. Philip Jenkins, *God's Continent* (New York: Oxford University Press, 2007), 108.

127. George W. Braswell Jr., *Islam: Its Prophet, Peoples, Politics, and Power* (Nashville: Broadman & Holman, 1996), 35.

128. Ibid., 36.

129. Daniel Clendenin, *Eastern Orthodox Christianity* (Grand Rapids, Mich.: Baker, 1994), 40.

130. Ibid., 41.

131. Ibid.

132. Timothy Ware, *The Orthodox Church* (Baltimore: Penguin Books, 1964), 59.

133. Ibid., 40.

134. Nicolas Zernov, *Moscow the Third Rome* (New York: AMS, 1937), 15.

135. Clendenin, *Eastern,* 38.

136. Zernov, *Moscow,* 17.

137. Ibid., 36.

138. Clendenin, *Eastern,* 19.

139. St. John of Damascus, *On the Divine Images* (trans. David Anderson; Crestwood, N.Y.: St. Vladimir's Seminary Press, 1980), 60.

140. Ware, *The Orthodox Church,* 1.

141. Ibid., 204.

142. Ibid., 205.

143. Ibid.

144. Clendenin, *Eastern,* 50.

145. Wayne Grudem, *Bible Doctrine: Essential Teachings of the Christian Faith* (Grand Rapids, Mich.: Zondervan, 1999), 25.

146. Ibid., 55.

147. Ware, *The Orthodox Church,* 217.

148. Clendenin, *Eastern,* 56.

149. Ibid.

150. John of Damascus, *St. John of Damascus: Writings* (trans. F. H. Chase; Crestwood, N.Y.: St Vladimir's Seminary Press, 1958).

151. Timothy Ware, *The Orthodox Way* (Crestwood, N.Y.: St Vladimir's Orthodox Theological Seminary, 1979), 5.

152. Ibid., 28–29.

153. Ibid., 43.

154. Ibid., 58.

155. Ibid., 83.

156. Ibid., 121–122.

157. Ibid., 140.

158. Ibid., 184.

159. Nathaniel Davis, *A Long Walk to Church* (Cambridge, Mass.: Westview Press, 2003), 13.

160. Preston Pearce, interviewed by author, 12 November 2010.

161. Everett Gill, letter to Charles Maddry, March 30, 1938, archives.

162. Charles Maddry, *The Commission,* April 1942, archives.

163. B. H. Liddell Hart, *History of the Second World War* (New York: Putnam's Sons, 1971), 6.

164. Ibid.

165. Ibid., 16.

166. Ibid.

167. Ibid., 393.

168. Obituary of Everett Gill, February 1958, Raleigh, NC.

169. Everett Gill, letter to Charles Maddry, March 30, 1938, archives.

170. Minutes of the Foreign Mission Board of the SBC, Trustee Meeting, December 22, 1941, archives.

171. Ibid.

172. *The Commission,* January 1942, archives.

173. Earl Hester Trutza, *The Commission,* July–August 1941, archives.

174. Minutes of the Foreign Mission Board of the SBC, Annual SBC Convention, May 14, 1941, archives.

175. Ibid.

176. Minutes of the Foreign Mission Board of the SBC, Trustee Meeting, December 11, 1941, archives.

177. Minutes of the Foreign Mission Board of the SBC, Annual SBC Convention,

May 16, 1944, archives.

178. Minutes of the Foreign Mission Board of the SBC, Annual SBC Conference, February 6, 1945, archives.

179. Minutes of the Foreign Mission Board of the SBC, Trustee Meeting, October 9, 1945, archives.

180. Ibid.

181. Minutes of the Foreign Mission Board of the SBC, Annual SBC Convention, May 14, 1941, archives.

182. Minutes of the Foreign Mission Board of the SBC, Trustee Meeting, January 8, 1942, archives.

183. Minutes of the Foreign Mission Board of the SBC, Annual SBC Convention, May 15, 1946, archives.

184. Ibid.

185. Minutes of the Foreign Mission Board of the SBC, Trustee Meeting, July 10, 1947, archives.

186. Minutes of the Foreign Mission Board of the SBC, Annual SBC Convention, May 14, 1941, archives.

187. Pauline Moore, interviewed by author, 25 July 2010.

188. Keith Parker, interviewed by author, 10 March 2007.

189. Minutes of the Foreign Mission Board of the SBC, Trustee Meeting, January 8, 1942, archives.

190. Moore, interview.

191. Minutes of the Foreign Mission Board of the SBC, Trustee Meeting, April 10, 1945, archives.

192. Minutes of the Foreign Mission Board of the SBC, Trustee Meeting, October 9, 1945, archives.

193. Ibid.

194. Minutes of the Foreign Mission Board of the SBC, Annual SBC Convention, May 13, 1948, archives.

195. Minutes of the Foreign Mission Board of the SBC, Trustee Meeting, January 13, 1949, archives.

196. Minutes of the Foreign Mission Board of the SBC, Trustee Meeting, September 8, 1949, archives.

197. Minutes of the Foreign Mission Board of the SBC, Annual SBC Convention, May 14, 1952, archives.

198. Minutes of the Foreign Mission Board of the SBC, Trustee Meeting, September 8, 1949, archives.

199. Ibid.

200. Ibid.

201. Minutes of the Foreign Mission Board of the

SBC, Trustee Meeting, October 14, 1952, archives.

202. Pollock, *The Faith,* 87.

203. Sawatsky, *Soviet Evangelicals,* 131.

204. Davis, *A Long Walk to Church,* 34.

205. Sawatsky, *Soviet Evangelicals,* 152.

206. Ibid., 177.

207. Corrado and Pilli, *Eastern European Baptist History,* 123–24.

208. David A. Noebel, *Understanding the Times* (Manitou Springs, Colo.: Summit Press, 1991), acknowledgments.

209. Ibid.

210. *Encyclopedia Americana,* "Communism," 7:435.

211. V. I. Lenin, *Complete Collected Works* (45 vols.; Moscow: Progress Publishers, 1978), vol. 15, 402.

212. Ibid., 405.

213. Noebel, *Understanding,* 73.

214. Sawatsky, *Soviet Evangelicals,* 263.

215. Ibid., 435.

216. Nela Williams Mayer, interview.

217. Minutes of the Foreign Mission Board of the SBC, Trustee Meeting, June 29, 1976, archives.

218. John David Hopper, interviewed by author, 22 April 2010.

219. Jim Smith, interviewed by editor, 23 April 2012.

220. Minutes of the Foreign Mission Board of the SBC, Trustee Meeting, February 10, 1986, archives.

221. Minutes of the Foreign Mission Board of the SBC, Trustee Meeting, July 16, 1988, archives.

222. Don Martin, "Parks Calls 70-30 Ratio Effort to Speed Up World Evangelization," *Baptist Press* (July 27, 1988): 1. Sometimes written "70/30" and sometimes "70-30."

223. Ibid.

224. Jim Smith, interview by editor.

225. Philip Jenkins, *God's Continent,* 26.

226. Jose Casanova, "Religion, European Secular Identities and European Integration," *Religion in the New Europe* (ed. Krzysztof Michalski; New York: Central European University Press, 2006), 23.

227. Ibid., 25.

228. Ibid.

229. Houssain Kettani, "Muslim Population in Europe: 1950–2020," *International Journal of Environmental Science and Development* (June 2010): 154–164. [Cited 1 December 2010]. Online: http://www.ijesd.org/papers/29-D438.pdf.

230. Ibid.

231. Braswell, *Islam,* 205.

232. Ibid.

233. Ibid.

234. Clendenin, *Eastern,* 38.

235.235 Martha Skelton, "Soviet Union: When Will the Bells Ring Again?" *The Commission* (September 1988): 13.

236. Davis, *A Long Walk to Church,* 68.

237. Ibid., 68.

238. Minutes of the Foreign Mission Board of the SBC, Trustee Meeting, July 21, 1990, archives.

239. Ibid.

240. Ibid.

241. Ibid.

242. Ibid.

243. Minutes of the Foreign Mission Board of the SBC, Trustee Meeting, December 9, 1991, archives.

244. Ibid.

245. FMB Trustees determined that the International Baptist Theological Seminary in Ruschlikon was too liberal and did not represent the theological position of the SBC. This decision led to the withdrawal of previously approved budget funds.

246. Keith Parks, interviewed by author, 30 December 2010.

247. Martha Skelton, "Reflecting on a Missions Career," *The Commission* (October/November 1988): 38.

248. Parks, interview.

249. Sam James, interviewed by author, 13 January 2011.

250. Keith Jones, *The European Baptist Federation: A Case Study in European Baptist Interdependency 1950-2006,* Colorado Springs, Colo.: Paternoster, 2009), 139.

251. James, interview.

252. Ibid.

253. Ibid., see Appendix 4.

254. Ibid.

255. Ibid.

256. Jim Smith, interviewed by author, 23 February 2010.

257. Jerry Rankin, interviewed by author, 16 December 2010.

258. Roger Briggs, interviewed by author, 16 December 2010.

259. John Floyd, interviewed by author, 19 May 2010.

260. Minutes of the Foreign Mission Board of the SBC, Trustee Meeting, April 27, 1994, archives.

261. Mike Creswell, "Europe, Middle East Baptist Leaders Confer with IMB on Unfinished Task," *Baptist Press* (April 11, 2000): 1.

262. Ibid.

263. John S. Leonard, "The Church Between Cultures: Rethinking the Church in Light of the Globalization of Immigration," n.p. [cited 17 January 2011]. Online: http://www.wts.edu.

264. Boyd Hatchel, interviewed by author, 16 December 2010.

265. The following countries emerged: Slovenia (1991), Croatia (1991), Macedonia (1992), Bosnia and Herzegovina (1992), and Serbia, including Kosovo, along with Montenegro comprised Yugoslavia in 2000.

266. Nela Williams, interviewed by author, 26 June 2008.

267. Minutes of the Foreign Mission Board of the SBC, SBC Annual Meeting, May 16, 1923, archives.

268. Williams, interview.

269. Mike Creswell, "Nela Williams: Rolling with the Punches," *The Commission* (September 1988): 38.

270. Ibid.

271. Bill Steele, interviewed by author, 19 May 2010.

272. Ibid.

273. Ibid.

274. Ibid.

275. Ibid.

276. Ibid.

277. Ibid.

278. Ibid.

279. Randy Bell, interviewed by author, 8 May 2010.

280. Ibid.

281. John Floyd, interviewed by author, 19 May 2010.

282. Minutes of the Foreign Mission Board of the SBC, Trustee Meeting, October 6, 1996, archives.

283. Ibid.

284. Ibid.

285. Trey Atkins, interviewed by author, 16 December 2010.

286. Ibid.

287. Kyle Kirkpatrick, interviewed by author, 29 October 2010.

288. Ibid.

289. Bell, interview.

290. David S. Mason, *Revolution in East-Central Europe* (Boulder, Colo.: Westview Press, 1992), 136.

291. Bell, interview.

292. Ibid.

293. Ibid.

294. Atkins, interview.

295. Randy Covington, interviewed by author, 15 February 2010.

296. Ibid.

297. Mayer, interview.

298. Minutes, July 16, 1988.

299. Errol Simmons, interviewed by author, 16 December 2010.

300. Ibid.

301. Minutes of the Foreign Mission Board of the SBC, Trustee Meeting, April 2, 1990, archives.

302. Simmons, interview.

303. Isam Ballenger, interviewed by author, 13 December 2010.

304. Simmons, interview.

305. Ibid.

306. Steve Booth, interviewed by author, 17 November 2010.

307. Partnership agreements between Baptist state conventions and Eastern European Baptist unions were very popular in the 1990s and usually formalized a three- to five-year relationship. Generally the state convention would send multiple volunteer teams over that time span to engage in priority union projects.

308. Booth, interview.

309. Simmons, interview.

310. Mike Creswell, "English-language Churches: Changing with the Times," *The Commission* (September 1988): 58.

311. Simmons, interview.

312. Booth, interview.

313. Ibid.

314. Mark Aderholt, interviewed by author, 3 January 2011.

315. Ibid.

316. Ibid.

317. Ibid.

318. Ibid.

319. Atkins, interview

320. T. Thomas, interviewed by author, 3 January 2011.

321. Ibid.

322. Ibid.

323. Ibid.

324. The Cooperative Baptist Fellowship is a sub-group of Southern Baptists that opposed the direction of the SBC following the contracted controversy of the 1980s related to the inerrancy of Scripture and other issues.

325. Bill Richardson, interviewed by author, 16 December 2010.

326. Minutes of the Foreign Mission Board of the SBC, Annual SBC Convention, May 16, 1923, archives.

327. Richardson, interview.

328. Ibid.

329. Vesta Sauter, interviewed by author, 14 December 2010.

330. Ibid.

331. Ibid.

332. Hatchel, interview.

333. Pearce, interview.

334. Larry Carnes, interviewed by author, 17 November 2010.

335. Ibid.

336. Pearce, interview.

337. Carnes, interview.

338. Hatchel, interview.

339. Carnes, interview.

340. George Lozuk, interviewed by author, 11 February 2010.

341. Ballenger, interview.

342. Lozuk, interview.

343. Mel Skinner, interviewed by author, 8 February 2010.

344. Ibid.

345. Minutes of the Foreign Mission Board of the SBC, Trustee Meeting, December 7, 1992, archives.

346. Ibid.

347. Bob Tucker, interviewed by author, 7 February 2010.

348. Skinner, interview.

349. Ibid.

350. Perry Glanzer, "A Troubled Troika: The CoMission, the Russian Ministry of Education, and the Russian Orthodox Church," *East-West Church & Ministry Report* 8, no. 3 (Summer 2000): 1.

351. Ibid.

352. Ibid.

353. Norman Lytle, interviewed by author, 30 December 2010.

354. Connie Robbins, interviewed by author, 1 February 2010.

355. Ibid.

356. Don Martin, "Khabarovsk Baptists Plan Memorial for Slain Southern Baptist Couple," *Baptist Press* (March 31, 1995): 1.

357. Mark Elliott, "Two Missionaries Murdered in Russia," *East-West Church & Ministry Report* 3, no. 2 (Spring 1995): 4.

358. Martin, "Khabarovsk," 1.

359. Elliott, "Two Missionaries," 4.

360. Ibid.

361. Robbins, interview.

362. Ibid.

363. Ibid.

364. Ibid.

365. Covington, interviewed by author, 15 February 2010.

366. Ibid.

367. Paul Babb, interview.

368. Ibid.

369. Ibid.

370. Martha Skelton, "Living Faith in the Land of Exile," *The Commission* (May/June 1994): 10.

371. Ibid., 26.

372. Ibid., 13.

373. Charles Hardie, interviewed by author, 23 December 2010.

374. Ibid.

375. Ibid.

376. Minutes of the Foreign Mission Board of the SBC, Trustee Meeting, October 9, 1995, archives.

377. Skinner, interview.

378. Minutes, October 9, 1995.

379. Buck Burch, interviewed by author, 29 October 2010.

380. Ibid.

381. Erich Bridges, "Co-Laboring in the North," *The Commission* (Summer 2007): 47.

382. Burch, interview.

383. Ibid.

384. Ibid.

385. Chris Carr, interviewed by author, 14 January 2011.

386. Ed Tarleton, interviewed by author, 25 July 2010.

387. Bill Wardlaw, interviewed by author, 4 February 2010.

388. Mike Creswell, "Bulgaria: Hard Field for Baptists," *The Commission* (May/June 1994): 64.

389. Ibid.

390. Ibid.

391. Bruce Cassells, interviewed by author, 12 February 2010.

392. Ibid.

393. Wardlaw, interview.

394. Theo Angelov, "The Light of the Gospel during time of Persecution: The Baptist Churches in Bulgaria During the Time of Communism" (unpublished article for the Baptist Union of Bulgaria).

395. Spencer Stith, interviewed by author, 14 December 2010.

396. Ibid.

397. Roger Capps, interviewed by author, 20 December 2010.

398. Ibid.

399. Creswell, "Bulgaria," 65.

400. Wardlaw, interview.

401. Stith, interview.

402. Cassels, interview.

403. Smith, interviewed by author.

404. Minutes of the Foreign Mission Board of the SBC, Trustee Meeting, April 2, 1990, archives.

405. Tom Cleary, interviewed by author, 11 December 2010.

406. Smith, interview.

407. Konstanty Wiazowski, interviewed by author, 18 December 2010.

408. Ibid.

409. Martha Skelton, "Poland: New Day, New Opportunity," *The Commission* (March/April 1995): 44.

410. Minutes of the Foreign Mission Board of the SBC, Trustee Meeting, October 10, 1994, archives.

411. Gustaw Cieslar, interviewed by author, 18 December 2010.

412. Ibid.

413. Martha Skelton, "Poland: New Day, New Opportunity," 45.

414. Ibid., 46.

415. Ibid., 49.

416. Ibid., 53.

417. Sergiusz Borecki, interviewed by author, 15 October 2009.

418. Atkins, interview.

419. Mick Stockwell, interviewed by author, 15 September 2010.

420. Ibid.

421. Steve Haines, interviewed by author, 15 December 2010.

422. Ballenger, interview.

423. Gregory Kommendant, interviewed by author, 21 December 2010.

424. Stockwell, interview.

425. Floyd, interview.

426. Haines, interview.

427. Ibid.

428. Ibid.

429. Ibid.

430. Mike Norfleet, interviewed by author, 30 December 2010.

431. Ibid.

432. Haines, interview.

433. Stockwell, interview.

434. Ibid.

435. Stockwell, interview.

436. Dan Panter, interviewed by author, 1 November 2010.

437. Ibid.

438. Mike Creswell, "The Panters Lend a Hand," *The Commission* (January 1993): 41.

439. Ibid.

440. Andy Leininger, interviewed by author, 24 February 2010.

441. Ibid.

442. Ibid.

443. Bob Ford, interviewed by author, 11 February 2010.

444. Hugh LeCaine Agnew, *The Czechs and the Lands of the Bohemian Crown* (Stanford, Calif.: Hoover Institution Press, 2004), 284.

445. Ibid., 292.

446. Josef Solc, interviewed by author, 15 November 2010.

447. Ford, interview.

448. Ibid.

449. Mark Sauter, interviewed by author, 14 December 2010.

450. Ibid.

451. Mark Sauter, interview.

452. Ibid.

453. Ibid.

454. Craig Averill, interviewed by author, 21 December 2010.

455. Ibid.

456. Atkins, interview.

457. Hatchel, interview.

458. Atkins, interview

459. Tucker, interview.

460. Ibid.

461. Monte Erwin, interviewed by author, 15 February 2010.

462. Ibid.

463. Stockwell, interview.

464. Fred Ater, interviewed by author, 19 March 2010.

465. Ibid.

466. Ibid.

467. Ibid.

468. Ibid.

469. John H. Y. Briggs, ed., *A Dictionary of European Baptist Life and Thought* (Colorado Springs: Paternoster, 2009): 337.

470. Ken McLemore, interviewed by author, 17 January 2011.

471. Richard Bartels, interviewed by author, 6 January 2011.

472. Ibid.

473. Tom Fox, interviewed by author, 22 April 2010.

474. Ibid.

475. Ibid.

476. Ibid.

477. Ibid.

478. Ibid.

479. Ibid.

480. Ibid.

481. Stockwell, interview.

482. Michael Kort, *The Soviet Colossus* (6th ed.; Armonk, N.Y.: M. E. Sharpe, 2006), 400.

483. Milton Magalhaes, interviewed by author, 16 March 2010.

484. Ibid.

485. Ibid.

486. Ibid.

487. Ibid.

488. Ibid.

489. Mary Carpenter, letter to Kim P. Davis, 24 September 1992.

490. Briggs, *A Dictionary of European Baptist Life and Thought*, 4.

491. Ibid., 74.

492. Ibid.

493. Ibid.

494. Mary Carpenter, interviewed by editor, 1992.

495. David Carpenter, newsletter, 1992.

496. Mary Carpenter, interview.

497. Gerry Milligan, interviewed by author, 17 January 2011.

498. Ibid.

499. Ibid.

500. Ibid

501. Gale Hartley, interviewed by author, 7 December 2010.

502. Ibid.

503. Mike Creswell, "Albania Emerges from the Darkness," *The Commission* (September/October 1995): 44.

504. Ibid.

505. Marty Croll, "Albania's Respond to Film," *The Commission* (September/October 1994): 3.

506. Ibid.

507. David Carpenter, interviewed by author, 6 March 2012.

508. Charles Wiggs, interviewed by author, 10 January 2011.

509. Mary Carpenter, interview.

510. David Carpenter, newsletter, July 1996.

511. Minutes, October 9, 1995.

512. Hartley, interview.

513. Lee Bradley, interviewed by author, 17 February 2010.

514. Ibid.

515. Covington, interview.

516. Minutes of the Foreign Mission Board of the SBC, Trustee Meeting, April 2, 1990, archives.

517. Minutes of the Foreign Mission Board of the SBC, Trustee Meeting, August 12, 1991, archives.

518. Minutes, April 2, 1990.

519. Angelov, "The Light of the Gospel."

520. Minutes, April 2, 1990.

521. Lozuk, interview.

522. Fox, interview.

523. Martin, "Parks Calls 70-30 Ratio."

524. James, interview.

525. Ford, interview.

526. Mike Creswell, "Europe, Middle East Baptist Leaders Confer with IMB on Unfinished Task," *Baptist Press* (April 11, 2000): 1.

527. Ibid.

528. Pearce, interview.

529. "Europe's Mujahideen: Where Mass Immigration Meets Global Terrorism," n.p. [cited 17 January 2011], Online: http://www.cis.org.

530. Kenneth R. Ross, "Non-Western Christians in Scotland: Missions in Reverse," n.p. [cited 20 January 2011]. Online: http://www.ctbi.org.uk.

531. Jan A. B. Jongeneel, "The Mission of Migrant Churches in Europe" (paper presented at the annual meeting of the American Society of Missiology, Techny, Ill., 20-22 June 2003), 29-33.

532. Ibid., 32.

533. Ibid.

534. Ibid.

535. Atkins, interview.

536. Stockwell, interview.

537. Ibid.

538. Hopper, interview.

539. Ibid.

540. Ibid.

541. Lozuk, interview.

542. James, interview.

543. Ballenger, interview.

544. Steele, interview.

545. Ballenger, interview.

546. John Deal, interviewed by author, 21 November 2010.

547. Ibid.

548. James, interview.

549. Minutes of the Foreign Mission Board of the SBC, Trustee Meeting, October 6, 1996, archives.

550. Deal, interview.

551. Rankin, interview.

552. Minutes of the Foreign Mission Board of the SBC, Trustee Meeting, February 12, 1990, archives.

553. Ibid.

554. Ibid.

555. Ballenger, interview.

556. Ibid.

557. Larry Cox, interviewed by author, 14 January 2011.

558. Clark Braun (pseudonym), interviewed by author, 29 January, 2010.

559. Rankin, interview.

560. IMB research department.

561. Wardlaw, interview.

562. Panter, interview.

563. James, interview.

564. Panter, interview.

565. Hatchel, interview.

566. Tucker, interview.

567. Burch, interviewed by author, 29 October 2010.

568. Bradley, interview.

569. Minutes, April 2, 1990.

570. Ibid.

571. Ibid.

572. Ibid.

573. Burch, interview.

574. Panter, interview.

575. Minutes of the Foreign Mission Board of the SBC, Trustee Meeting, June 7, 1996, archives.

576. Don Hinkle, "SBC Severs Ties with BWA as Theological Concerns Remain," *Baptist Press* (June 15, 2004): 1.

577. Greg Warner, "Leaders Predict SBC Backed Network Won't Find Acceptance in Europe," *Associated Baptist Press* (August 11, 2005): 1.

578. Wiazowski, interview.

579. Minutes of the Foreign Mission Board of the SBC, Trustee Meeting, October 9, 1945, archives.

580. Panter, interview.

581. Erwin, interview.

582. Atkins, interview.

583. Booth, interview.

584. Wiazowski, interview.

585. Minutes, June 7, 1996.

586. Ibid.

587. Kommendant, interview.

588. Magalhaes, interview.

589. Braun, interview.

590. Bradley, interview.

591. Ibid.

592. Names withheld for security reasons.

593. Mayer, interview.

594. Parker, interview.

595. Ballenger, interview.

596. James, interview.

597. Stockwell, interview.

598. Ballenger, interview.

599. Ibid.

600. Mike Creswell, "Europe, Middle East Baptist Leaders Confer," 1.

601. Stockwell, interview.

602. Rankin, interview.

603. Stockwell, interview.